LANCASTER PAMPHLETS

Stalin and Stalinism

Second Edition

Alan Wood

 Routledge
Taylor & Francis Group

LONDON AND NEW YORK

First published 1990
by Routledge
2 Park Square, Milton Park, Abingdon, Oxon, OX14 4RN

Simultaneously published in the USA and Canada
by Routledge
270 Madison Ave, New York, NY 10016

Second edition published 2005

Routledge is an imprint of the Taylor & Francis Group

© 1990, 2005 Alan Wood

Typeset in Bembo by Graphicraft Limited, Hong Kong
Printed and bound in Great Britain by
TJ International Ltd, Padstow, Cornwall

British Library Cataloguing in Publication Data
A catalogue record for this book is available from the British Library

Library of Congress Cataloging in Publication Data

Wood, Alan, 1943–
Stalin and Stalinism / Alan Wood.—2nd ed.
p. cm. – (Lancaster pamphlets)
Includes bibliographical references and index.
1. Stalin, Joseph, 1879–1953. 2. Heads of state—Soviet Union—
Biography. 3. Soviet Union—Politics and government—1917–1936.
4. Soviet Union—Politics and government—1936–1953.
I. Title. II. Series.

DK268.S8W63 2004
947.084′2′092—dc22
[B]
2004051079

ISBN 0–415–30732–5 (pbk)
ISBN 0–415–30731–7 (hbk)

Contents

Foreword

Lancaster Pamphlets offer concise and up-to-date accounts of major historical topics, primarily for the help of students preparing for Advanced Level examinations, though they should also be of value to those pursuing introductory courses in universities and other institutions of higher education. Without being all-embracing, their aims are to bring some of the central themes or problems confronting students and teachers into sharper focus than the textbook writer can hope to do; to provide the reader with some of the results of recent research which the textbook may not embody; and to stimulate thought about the whole interpretation of the topic under discussion.

Author's preface

This pamphlet was originally written during March 1989, before the full extent of the dramatic revolutionary changes which shook Eastern Europe at the end of that year could have been fully anticipated. One by one, the Communist governments of that region were forced from office by mass popular upheavals; the most potent symbol of the post-war division of Europe, the Berlin Wall, was torn down, and events moved rapidly towards the reunification of the two Germanys; heads of government, presidents and Communist Party leaders throughout the region – people who had made their careers by serving the system originally imposed on their countries by Joseph Stalin during the Cold War – were sacked, humiliated, arrested and, in the case of Romania's Nicolae Ceaușescu, shot.

Over the next two years (1989–91) the Soviet Union itself experienced a period of acute economic, social and political turmoil that eventually led to the collapse of the USSR; the abolition of the Soviet Communist Party and the ignominious removal of its General Secretary, Mikhail Gorbachev; the territorial dismemberment of the country into a loose confederation of independent republics – the Commonwealth of Independent States (CIS); the disappearence of the Eastern bloc's military organization, the Warsaw Pact; economic chaos and ethnic tensions within and among the former Soviet Republics, which in many cases led to bloody, and still continuing, civil wars.

All of those events and movements represent aspects of the death of a system established in the USSR by the once Soviet dictator, Joseph Stalin, the subject of this brief study. That is why, to understand the significance of recent and current upheavals, which have global ramifications, it is essential to understand the political, historical, and ideological phenomena signified by the title of this booklet – *Stalin and Stalinism.*

Alan Wood
Lancaster, 1994

Preface to the second edition

In the year 1903, a new word entered the political vocabulary of the world. That word was 'Bolshevik'. In modern English usage, its contracted form 'bolshie' is popularly applied to a person whose behaviour is considered to be deliberately awkward, contumacious or uncooperative. The original Russian term (derived from the Russian word for 'majority') was coined by Lenin to refer to his hard-line faction of supporters at the Second Congress of the Russian Social Democratic Labour Party. The split between the Bolsheviks and their opponents within the Party, the Mensheviks (i.e. members of the 'minority'), arose initially over questions of party membership, organization and discipline. And it was the supposedly organized, disciplined Bolsheviks who were to seize political power in Russia during the October 1917 Revolution and lay the foundations of the Union of Soviet Socialist Republics (USSR).

Exactly fifty years after the term first gained currency, the man who was to distort the Bolsheviks' grandiose vision of international socialist revolution into one of the twentieth century's most brutal dictatorships died in his country cottage near Moscow. That man was Joseph Vissarionovich Stalin (born Iosif Djugashvili, 1879–1953). At the time of writing, then, one hundred years have elapsed since the birth of Bolshevism, and fifty years since the death of Stalin. It therefore seems to be an appropriate time to reconsider the legacy of Stalin and Stalinism, taking into account some of the historical re-thinking that has taken place both in Russia and the West over

xi

the past half century, and particularly since the collapse of the Soviet Union in 1991.

In the preface to the 1994 reprint of this Pamphlet (p. xix, here reproduced on p. ix), attention was drawn to the whirlwind of events, which, following Mikhail Gorbachev's attempts to introduce wide-ranging economic, structural and cultural reform under the slogans of *perestroika* (restructuring) and *glasnost* (openness, freedom of expression), the once-mighty Soviet empire suddenly disintegrated and all but disappeared. One of the reasons for this dramatic up-heaval was the incompatibility between introducing 'new thinking', new practices and a new approach to international relations within the confines of a one-party state in which the monopoly of political power was still invested in the Communist Party of the Soviet Union (CPSU). As the population began to exercise its new-found freedoms, as the Soviet republics clamoured for greater independ-ence and as the people of the satellite states of Eastern Europe gradually tore themselves away from the grip of Russian domination, so did the whole political and historical legitimacy of the Soviet system get called into question. That system, both its institutions and its ideology, was essentially the product of the policies doggedly pursued and ruthlessly implemented during the quarter-century of Stalin's iron rule between 1928 and 1953, and continued in rather less tyrannical fashion by his successors.

Although the contours of international relations have altered in dramatic and violent ways in the early years of the present century, Russia still occupies a prominent place on the political map of planet Earth, and both the domestic and foreign policies of President Vladimir Putin need to be taken careful account of by the world's statesmen. He himself is an ex-Communist Party member, a former KGB offi-cer and a product of the authoritarian Soviet system, albeit in its dying days. Under his regime, despite the growth of obscene wealth in some quarters, nearly half the population of the Russian Federation lives beneath the official poverty line. Putin still pursues a vicious internal war against Chechnya in which thousands have perished. Hundreds of ordinary Russian citizens have died of terrorist attacks in apartment blocks, public buildings, the theatre and the Moscow underground. Perhaps most shockingly, the massacre of around 300 children and adults at a school in Beslan, North Ossetia, in September 2004 is a dreadful reminder of the terrifying national, political, ethnic and religious tensions which are a remaining legacy of Russia's imperial and Stalinist past. The government still has a near total monopoly of the media and channels of public information. Environmental pollution is out of control. Life expectancy is among the lowest in the developed world. There is little genuine democracy, and crime and corruption are rampant. And yet Putin remains a massively popular leader, winning a landslide victory in the March 2004 presidential elections. If there is something of a paradox here in explaining the popularity of a president whose policies are so manifestly unsuccessful, how much more complex a problem it is to understand how Joseph Stalin clung on to power for so long, terrorizing the population, resorting to mass murder and genocide, running a government based on sycophancy, falsehood and fear, and all but enslaving the nations of Eastern Europe. At the same time he was genuinely admired, revered, even loved, by many, and there are still those today who entertain a misplaced affection and nostalgia for his era.

For historians of twentieth-century Russia, the task of unravelling the enigma of Stalin remains one of their thorniest problems. The aim of this second edition is to make a modest contribution to the debate in the light of more up-to-date research and revisionist theories concerning one of modern history's most fascinating and fearsome figures.

Where appropriate, short additions and elaborations have been interpolated into the original text, while some chapters have been more extensively revamped in order to incorporate new material or develop earlier arguments. An attempt has been made to give rather more emphasis to the social and cultural aspects of Stalinism, as well as such topics as Stalin's role in the Civil War, the conduct of the purges and the 'Great Terror', the 'intentionalist' versus 'structuralist' debate, and the Cold War. A new section of biographical notes has been appended, and the 'Suggestions for further reading' re-designed and selectively updated.

Alan Wood
Lancaster, 2004

Notes and acknowledgements

Russian personal names that are more familiar in their anglicized version have been rendered accordingly; otherwise they have been retained in their original form. This accounts for such apparent inconsistencies as Tsar *Nicholas* I and *Nikolai* Bukharin; Grand Duke *Michael*, but *Mikhail* Gorbachev.

In the transliteration of Russian technical terms, acronyms, abbreviations and surnames, a common-sense pattern has been adopted that combines certain features of the standard systems.

Dates before February 1918 are given according to the Julian calendar, until then used in Russia. Thereafter they follow the Gregorian calendar.

St Petersburg was the name of the capital of the Russian Empire until 1914. During the First World War its name was changed to its Russian form – Petrograd. In 1918 Moscow became the new capital, and in 1924 Petrograd was renamed Leningrad. (In 1992 it reverted to its original name, St Petersburg.)

No attempt has been made to psychoanalyse Stalin's character and behaviour, and no details are given about his personal relationships and family life.

The drafts of the earlier edition and reprints of this pamphlet were read and commented on by Dr Mike Perrins and my former student, Terry Cocks. My wife, Iris, and my younger daughter, Tanya, also helped in various ways. The text of this new edition has been carefully scrutinized by my colleague and teaching assistant, Dr John Swift, to whom much thanks. Thanks, too, to Gillian Oliver, formerly of Routledge, for suggesting the new version, and to Alex Ballantine, Development Editor, for coaxing it, and me, along. My close friend, Dr Sergei Savoskul of the Russian Academy of Sciences in Moscow, has also been a constant support in my study of his country over many years.

Chronological guide

Unless otherwise specifically stated, all entries refer to the life and activities of Stalin.

1879
9 Dec.   Born in Gori, Georgia.
1888
Sept.   Begins local elementary school.
1894
Sept.   Enters Tiflis Orthodox Theological Seminary.
1898   Joins Georgian Marxist political circle, *Messame Dassy*. Founding Congress of Russian Social Democratic Workers' Party (RSDRP) in Minsk.
1899   Expelled from seminary.
1902   Arrested in Batumi for revolutionary activities; exiled to Siberia.
1903   Second Congress of RSDRP; split occurs between Mensheviks and Lenin's Bolsheviks.
1904   Escapes from Siberia and returns to Transcaucasia.
1905   Revolutionary upheavals throughout Russian Empire.
Dec.   Attends Bolshevik Conference in Finland; meets Lenin for the first time.
1906–12   Active in revolutionary underground; several times arrested, imprisoned, and exiled; present at 1906 and 1907 congresses of RSDRP.

1912
Jan.   Prague Congress of RSDRP; split between
            Mensheviks and Bolsheviks becomes final; Stalin
            not present, but made member of Bolshevik
            Central Committee.
Sept.   Escapes from exile.
Sept.–Dec. Edits *Pravda*; visits Lenin in Cracow, Poland.
1913
Jan.   Writes first major theoretical work, *Marxism and
            the National Problem*, on Lenin's suggestion.
Feb.   Returns to St Petersburg; re-arrested.
July.   Exiled to Siberia again.
1913–17   Remains in Siberian exile.
1914   Outbreak of First World War.
1917
Feb.–March February Revolution; abdication of Tsar Nicholas
            II; formation of first Provisional Government and
            Petrograd Soviet of Workers' and Soldiers' Deputies.
March   Returns from exile; rejoins editorial board of
            Pravda.
April   Lenin returns to Russia from exile in Switzerland.
July   Lenin avoids arrest and goes into hiding in
            Finland. Stalin becomes Bolsheviks' leading
            spokesman on Petrograd Soviet and member of
            party's new Central Committee.
Oct.   Bolsheviks seize power and form Soviet of
            People's Commissars; Stalin becomes Commissar
            for Nationalities.
1918
Jan.–March Supports Lenin's attempts to conclude peace with
            Germany.
March   Treaty of Brest-Litovsk signed. Civil War gets
            under way.
June–Oct.   In Tsaritsyn on political mission; clashes with local
            military commander and with Commissar for
            War, Trotsky.
1919   RSDRP renamed the All-Russian Communist
            Party (Bolsheviks); Stalin elected to Politburo and
            Orgburo.
March   First Congress of Communist International,
            Moscow.

Oct.–Dec.	Defeat of White forces in south and Siberia; Stalin active on various military fronts.
1921	Tenth Party Congress; inauguration of New Economic Policy.
	Stalin preoccupied with nationalities policies; crushes independent Georgian government.
1922	
April	Appointed General Secretary of Party Central Committee.
May	Lenin suffers first stroke.
Sept.–Dec.	Lenin quarrels with Stalin over handling of nationalities issue.
Dec.	Formation of Union of Soviet Socialist Republics (USSR).
1923	
Jan.	Lenin proposes Stalin's removal from post of General Secretary; suffers second stroke, retires from political life.
1924	
21 Jan.	Death of Lenin. Stalin in charge of funeral arrangements.
April	Publication of *Foundations of Leninism*. Beginnings of the 'cult of Lenin'.
May–Dec.	Anti-Trotsky campaign gathers pace.
1925–6	Develops theory of 'Socialism in One Country'; campaign against Trotsky widens to include Kamenev and Zinoviev.
1927	Trotsky and Zinoviev expelled from the party.
1928	Visits western Siberia and orders forcible requisitioning of grain.
	Inauguration of first five-year plan for the rapid industrialization of the economy.
1929	Announces full-scale collectivization of agriculture; refers to 'liquidation of the kulaks'.
1930	Publication of article, 'Dizzy with Success', criticizing over-zealous collectivization methods.
1932	First five-year plan completed in four years.
	Formula of 'socialist realism' in literature adopted.
1933	Adolf Hitler becomes Chancellor of Germany.
	Famine in Ukraine.

1934	
Jan.–Feb.	Seventeenth Party Congress – 'Congress of Victors'. Yagoda becomes head of NKVD.
1 Dec.	Assassination of Kirov heralds beginning of purge.
1935	Kamenev and Zinoviev arrested in connection with Kirov's murder. Adoption of policy of Popular Fronts against fascism in Europe.
1936	The 'Great Terror' gets under way.
June	Public show trial, conviction, and execution of Kamenev, Zinoviev, and others.
Aug.	Yezhov replaces Yagoda as head of NKVD.
Nov.	Publication of new Constitution of USSR, proclaimed as 'the most democratic in the world'.
1937	Height of the terror; second major show trial and execution of the accused; purge of the officer corps of Soviet armed forces. End of second five-year plan.
1938	
March	Trial and execution of Bukharin and others.
Oct.	Munich agreement on dismemberment of Czechoslovakia.
Dec.	Beria replaces Yezhov as head of NKVD.
1939	
March	Purges declared to be over.
Sept.	Germany invades Poland; beginning of Second World War in Europe. Soviet troops occupy eastern Poland.
Nov.	Soviet Union attacks Finland; start of the 'Winter War'.
1940	Stalin becomes Chairman of Council of People's Commissars (head of government).
March	End of war with Finland.
July	Soviet occupation of the Baltic states.
20 Aug.	Assassination of Trotsky in Mexico by Stalin's agent.
1941	
22 June	Operation Barbarossa – German invasion of USSR.
Oct.	Siege of Leningrad commences; battle for Moscow launched.
Dec.	Soviet counter-offensive; Moscow saved.

1942

June–Aug.	Soviet forces retreat in south; battle of Stalingrad commences.
Nov.	Soviet troops cut off German 6th Army at Stalingrad.

1943

Jan.	Relief of Leningrad.
Feb.	Germans surrender at Stalingrad.
March	Stalin assumes rank of Marshal.
Nov.	Kiev retaken by Red Army. Teheran Conference (Stalin, Roosevelt, Churchill).

1944

June	Allied landings in Normandy.
July–Dec.	Soviet forces advance across eastern and south-eastern Europe.

1945

Jan.	Red Army enters Warsaw.
Feb.	Yalta Conference (Stalin, Roosevelt, Churchill).
May	Red Army reaches Berlin.
8/9 May	Germany surrenders; end of war in Europe.
June	Stalin adopts title of Generalissimo.
July–Aug.	Potsdam Conference (Stalin, Truman, Attlee).
6 Aug.	USA drops atomic bomb on Hiroshima.
8 Aug.	USSR declares war on Japan.
9 Aug.	Atomic bomb dropped on Nagasaki.
2 Sept.	End of war with Japan (no formal peace treaty signed between USSR and Japan).

1946

March	Announcement of fourth five-year plan for national reconstruction. Churchill's 'Iron Curtain' speech at Fulton, Missouri.
Aug.	'Zhdanov decrees' on literary and cultural conformity.

1948

June	Beginning of the Berlin blockade. Break between USSR and Yugoslavia.
Aug.	Death of Zhdanov; beginning of the 'Leningrad Affair'.

1949	
April	Establishment of North Atlantic Treaty Organization (NATO).
Oct.	Victory of Chinese communists; establishment of People's Republic of China.
Dec.	Stalin's seventieth birthday celebrated with lavish festivities.
1952	Nineteenth Party Congress.
1953	
Jan.	Discovery of so-called 'Doctors' Plot'.
5 March	Death of Stalin.
Sept.	USSR announces possession of the H-bomb.
1953–6	Period of 'Collective Leadership'.
1956	
Feb.	Twentieth Party Congress; Khrushchev denounces Stalin's 'cult of personality' in 'secret speech'.
1961	
Oct.	Twenty-second Party Congress; 'de-Stalinization' campaign at its height; Stalin's body removed from mausoleum.
1964	
Oct.	Khrushchev removed from power.
1964–82	General Secretaryship of Leonid Brezhnev, referred to in the former USSR as the 'era of stagnation'; criticism of Stalin muted.
1985	Mikhail Gorbachev becomes General Secretary of Soviet Communist Party; launches campaign of *glasnost* and *perestroika*, including radical re-examination of Stalin era.
1989	Collapse of communist governments throughout eastern Europe.
1991	Gorbachev forced to resign from office; Communist Party abolished; USSR ceases to exist.

In 1937 a rabbit fled from Leningrad and crossed the border into Finland. The officer at border control asked him why he wished to enter Finland. 'Because in Russia they're arresting and killing all the camels.'
'But you're not a camel. You're a rabbit.'
'I know, but how do I prove it?'

Russian anecdote

Introduction

During the late 1980s, the world became familiar with two Russian terms which were adopted as the slogan and the watchword for the tremendous sea-change which affected and altered almost every facet of Soviet life. These were the Russian words *glasnost* and *perestroika*, the first meaning 'openness', 'frankness' or 'publicity', and the second meaning literally 'restructuring'. They began to be used with increasing frequency in connection with the programme of economic, political and cultural reform inaugurated in the former Soviet Union after Mikhail Sergeevich Gorbachev (1931–) became the General Secretary of the country's Communist Party in 1985 and its President in 1988. Because of the tremendous international power and importance of the Soviet Union, those changes had wide repercussions not only for the peoples of the USSR, but for the rest of the world as well. This is not the right place to discuss them, but what is important to realize is that what was actually being 'restructured', but ultimately dismantled, was essentially the political, social, economic and ideological system that was created by the man who ruled over the Soviet Union for twenty-five years (1928–53) as its unchallenged dictator – Joseph Stalin.

For a quarter of a century, the entire life of the largest country in the world, and of millions of its citizens, was dominated by a political leader who was once described by the Yugoslav communist, Milovan Djilas, as 'the greatest criminal in history' in whom was combined 'the criminal senselessness of a Caligula with the refinement

1

of a Borgia and the brutality of a Tsar Ivan the Terrible'. How was it that the initial enthusiasms and aspirations of the Russian Revolution in 1917, which promised a more just and humane society, became distorted into a totalitarian despotism which trampled on justice and humanity and plunged the Soviet Union into a nightmare of terror which reached almost genocidal proportions? Was Stalinism the logical and inevitable consequence of Lenin's original revolutionary policies or, on the contrary, was it a grotesque perversion of Bolshevism, and was Trotsky right in calling Stalin 'the gravedigger of the Revolution'? The impressive economic achievements of the Stalin era cannot be denied, turning Russia from an underdeveloped, peasant society into an industrial giant and a military superpower capable of withstanding the onslaught of Hitler's armies in 1941–45, and terrifying the West during the years of the Cold War. As Stalin himself remarked, he found the country with the wooden plough and left her with the atomic bomb. But all this was accomplished at a dreadful price in human misery and suffering. Could it have been achieved by any other means than the oppressive weapons of coercion and control which Stalin wielded through the apparatus of a police state? Were there other, alternative, paths of economic development? Were the famines and forced labour camps, the millions of exiles and executions necessary for the building of 'socialism in one country'? And how did one man come to wield such terrifying power over the Communist Party and the Soviet people?

For two generations it was impossible not only to answer, but even to ask, such questions inside the Soviet Union. Until nearly a decade after his death, Stalin's embalmed corpse lay next to that of Lenin in the mausoleum on Red Square, still an object of public veneration and pilgrimage even after the then Soviet leader, Nikita Sergeevich Khrushchev (1894–1971), had delivered his startling attack on his dead master in 1956. And it took another two and a half decades before the 'accursed questions' of the Soviet Union's Stalinist past could be properly investigated and opened up for public debate and professional examination by historians, politicians, journalists and creative writers without fear of official disapproval or worse. But after 1985, it was rare to pick up a serious newspaper, magazine or journal in the Soviet Union that did not contain somewhere in its pages an article either directly or indirectly concerned with some aspect of Stalin's savage regime or his ambiguous legacy. There developed a new atmosphere of intellectual curiosity, agonizing self-questioning, critical re-evaluation and often acrimonious accusation in an attempt to fill in the 'blank spots' in Russia's recent history, which previously would have been unthinkable. Encouraged by Gorbachev, people were no longer afraid to ask the questions, but even today no-one is yet really sure of the answers – not even the professional historians who formed the vanguard of the assault on the discredited official versions of the historical record. Because of the uncertainty, pedagogy and politics were driven into such an impasse that in 1988 Russian history examinations were cancelled in all Soviet schools. In the same year, a leading Moscow newspaper carried a cartoon in which schoolteacher, textbook in hand, asks a young pupil, 'Do you want to know what it says in the books, or do you want to know the truth?'

It was a fascinating time not only to be witnessing the terminal throes of what has recently been described as 'the last of the empires', but also to observe Russian history both in the making and the re-making. To re-emphasize an earlier point, the Soviet colossus that shattered and crumbled in 1991 was essentially Stalin's creation, though its foundations were laid in Lenin's Revolution. What follows is an attempt to suggest an answer to some of the questions posed above, and to examine the way in which the son of a poor, drunken Georgian cobbler came to be the ruler of a world super-power, and – with strong competition from Hitler – arguably the most despotic, malevolent and controversial political figure in the history of the twentieth century.

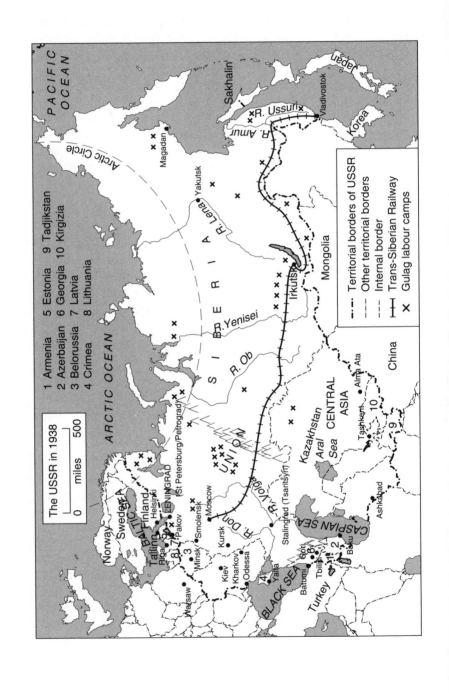

The USSR in 1938

1 Armenia	5 Estonia	9 Tadjikstan
2 Azerbaijan	6 Georgia	10 Kirgizia
3 Belorussia	7 Latvia	
4 Crimea	8 Lithuania	

0   miles   500

Territorial borders of USSR
Other territorial borders
Internal border
Trans-Siberian Railway
× Gulag labour camps

PACIFIC OCEAN
ARCTIC OCEAN
Arctic Circle

S I B E R I A

R. Lena
R. Yenisei
R. Ob
Irkutsk
Yakutsk
Magadan
Sakhalin'
R. Ussuri
R. Amur
Vladivostok
Korea
Mongolia
China

Norway
Sweden
Finland
Helsinki
BALTIC SEA
Tallinn
Riga
Pskov
LENINGRAD
(St Petersburg/Petrograd)
Moscow
Smolensk
Minsk
Warsaw
Kiev
Kharkov
Odessa
Kursk
U N I O N
R. Don
R. Volga
Stalingrad (Tsaritsyn)
BLACK SEA
Yalta
Batumi
Tbilisi
Baku
CASPIAN SEA
Turkey
Kazakhstan
Aral Sea
CENTRAL ASIA
Tashkent
Alma Ata
Ashkabad

1
The historical setting

Background

The internal social and economic conditions, the oppressive political system, the national tensions and the class conflicts within the Russian Empire which led to the revolution of 1917 have been described elsewhere in this series.* However, it is worth recalling some of the salient features of the tsarist social and political order into which Joseph Stalin was born and in which he served his revolutionary apprenticeship.

At the end of the nineteenth century, the Russian Empire was the largest continuous land-empire in the world, covering approximately one-sixth of the earth's land surface. In 1897 it contained a population of over 125 million people, of which only two-fifths were Russian. The other 60 per cent was made up of a multinational, multilingual and multireligious conglomeration of Slavs, Jews, Balts, Finns, Georgians, Armenians, Azeris, Turkic-speaking Muslim peoples of Central Asia, and a whole patchwork of aboriginal ethnic groups and tribes in Siberia and the Far East. Many of them suffered from various forms of racial discrimination and religious persecution and actively struggled to liberate themselves from Russian imperialism. Stalin, himself a

---

* Alan Wood, *The Origins of the Russian Revolution 1861–1917*, Lancaster Pamphlets, Routledge, London, 3rd edn, 2003.

non-Russian, made the nationalities problem of the Russian Empire one of his special areas of expertise, and it was in fact as People's Commissar for Nationalities that he made his political debut in the very first Soviet government.

From 1894 to 1917, this empire was ruled over by Tsar Nicholas II, the last representative of the Romanov dynasty, which had governed Russia for the past three centuries as absolute autocrats. Until as late as 1906 the country had neither parliamentary institutions nor legal political parties through which the will, or even the grievances, of the people could be expressed. Members of the government were appointed by the emperor and were directly responsible to his person; he consequently had the power to hire and fire them at will. There were no constitutional constraints on the tsar's authority and even the Fundamental Laws of the Russian Empire, which were promulgated after the revolutionary upheavals of 1905, stated unequivocally that the God-given supreme power lay with the Sovereign Autocrat. Russia therefore had a long and deeply ingrained tradition of political subservience to a single, all-powerful ruler. Many historians consider that this autocratic tradition, which in some ways Stalin inherited, had its roots in the imperial power-structure of the Byzantine Empire, from which Russia adopted its Orthodox Christianity, and in the 'oriental despotism' of the Mongol khans who occupied Russia in the early middle ages.

The overwhelming majority of Nicholas's subjects (over 80 per cent) were peasants, with only 13 per cent of the population living in towns or cities. Despite a remarkable burst of industrial growth at the turn of the century, Russia was still therefore an unmistakably agrarian society. Most of the peasants lived in village communes which closely regulated their activities and in many areas periodically redistributed land allotments among the peasant households. This redistributional system of land tenure and usage, combined with primitive farming techniques and a rapidly expanding rural population, led to agricultural underproduction, land hunger and occasional famine. The emancipation of the peasantry from serfdom in 1861 had miserably failed to solve the country's agrarian problems, and in the early years of the twentieth century there was a recrudescence of peasant violence that finally forced the government to introduce a new series of reforms in the village economy. The reforms were, however, 'too little and too late' and the rebellious peasantry continued to be a major thorn in the government's flesh before, during and until well after the 1917 Revolution. Stalin was later to tackle the peasant problem in his own inimical and inimitable manner, with devastating consequences.

Stalin's great rival, Lev Davidovich Trotsky (1879–1940), described the Russian peasantry as 'the subsoil of the Revolution'. The topsoil was provided by the industrial working class, or proletariat. Although only small in numbers compared with the peasants, the Russian workers had developed in a remarkably short period of time into a highly militant and class-conscious force in both economic and political terms. This was vividly demonstrated by the general strike of October 1905, which paralysed the country's economy and administration, and by the formation of the St Petersburg *Soviet* (Council) of workers' deputies, a kind of popular parliament that commanded the loyalty of the capital's workers in defiance of the bewildered government during the nationwide disorders of that year. The radicalization of the working class was partly a consequence of the appalling conditions in which they lived and worked, and partly a result of the propaganda and organization of Marxist revolutionary activists who welcomed the development of capitalist relationships in the Russian economy and looked beyond the overthrow of tsarism by a 'bourgeois-democratic revolution' to the time when the working class would rise and destroy capitalism and the bourgeois state in the inevitable 'proletarian-socialist revolution'.

In 1903 a newly formed underground revolutionary party, the Russian Social Democratic Workers' Party (RSDRP), had split into two mutually antagonistic factions known as the Bolsheviks ('majority-ites') and the Mensheviks ('minority-ites'). The Bolsheviks were led by Vladimir Ilyich Lenin (1870–1924), who in a pamphlet written in 1902, entitled *What's to be Done?*, had argued for a disciplined, centralized party organization of professional revolutionaries that would form the leadership – the 'vanguard' – of the proletariat in the socialist revolution. The Mensheviks, headed by Yulii Osipovich Martov (1873–1923), were in favour of a broader, mass party and generally held more moderate views on most practical and ideological issues than Lenin's hard-line Bolsheviks. It was of course the Bolsheviks who were to seize political power in the name of the workers' soviets in October 1917, and it was this party's bureaucratic machinery which was later to serve as the vehicle for Stalin's political ambition in his seemingly inexorable rise to supreme power during the 1920s. That process is examined in Chapter 3.

Revolution

The many conflicts and contradictions at work within the tsarist social and political structure were placed under intolerable strain as a result of Russia's entry into the First World War in August 1914. The short-lived jingoistic euphoria that initially greeted the declaration of hostilities rapidly gave way to a mood of frustration, despair and anger at the government's bungling mismanagement of the military and civilian war effort. Millions were conscripted and marched into the trenches of Eastern Europe with only a rudimentary training and often with inadequate weapons and ammunition. At the front, whole armies of these 'peasants in uniform' were defeated, decimated or taken as prisoners of war by the superior German and Austrian forces. In the rear, the unpopularity of the tsar and his government was exacerbated by Nicholas's foolish decision to take over personal command of the Russian army, and by the public scandal caused by the royal family's involvement in the sordid Rasputin affair. Members of the elected national assembly, the State Duma, called on the emperor to dismiss his incompetent ministers and replace them with a government that would enjoy the confidence of the people. Secret-police reports reinforced the politicians' fears with daily information of violent incidents on the streets and prophetic warnings about the increasingly revolutionary temper of the masses. Nicholas, however, paid no heed as the chorus of popular disaffection and war-weariness reached a dramatic crescendo in the early weeks of 1917.

At the end of February, striking workers, demonstrating women and mutinous soldiers held the capital in their grip and the authorities seemed powerless to re-establish order and control. The tsar, foiled by railway workers from returning to Petrograd (as St Petersburg had now been renamed) from army headquarters and faced with increasing pressure from his senior military advisers to step down, finally bowed to the inevitable and abdicated the throne in favour of his brother, Grand Duke Michael. Michael refused, and the three-hundred-year rule of the Romanov tsars was at a sudden end. The political vacuum created by the collapse of the autocracy was quickly, though confusingly, filled by the creation of two independent organs of authority, the self-styled Provisional Government, composed of moderate Duma politicians, and the Petrograd Soviet of Workers' and Soldiers' Deputies, which represented the interests of the revolutionary workers and troops of the capital. Similar soviets were soon established throughout the country, replacing in a somewhat anarchical fashion the now defunct authority of the imperial administration. This situation was later described by Lenin as one of 'dual power'.

The socialist parties, including both Bolsheviks and Mensheviks, naturally welcomed the collapse of tsarism as the predicted 'bourgeois-democratic revolution', and although their attitude to the relationship between the Provisional Government and the Petrograd Soviet was somewhat equivocal, none of the parties' leaders was yet thinking seriously about the possibility of a 'proletarian-socialist revolution' in the immediate future. Stalin was one of the first senior Bolsheviks to return to Petrograd from exile after the February Revolution, but it was really the arrival of Lenin on 3 April that introduced a new and ultimately decisive factor into the highly volatile political atmosphere. The Bolshevik leader announced that there should be no collaboration with the bourgeois government, no reunification of the Bolshevik and Menshevik parties, and no further participation by Russia in the imperialist war. He characterized the current situation as a period of transition from the bourgeois–democratic to the proletarian–socialist phase of the revolutionary process and called on the party to prepare the masses for an armed insurrection that would transfer 'all power to the soviets'. From early April, therefore, barely one month after the collapse of the Romanov autocracy, a workers' revolution, led by the Bolsheviks in the name of the Soviets, was squarely in Lenin's sights. His *April Theses*, as Lenin's proposals came to be called, were initially repudiated by other leading Bolsheviks, including Stalin, as not only premature, but even preposterous, but eventually became accepted as the Party's 'order of the day'.

It was not, however, for another six months that circumstances were deemed to be sufficiently favourable to put that order into effect. Only in September, after the collapse of two provisional governments, continuing military disasters at the front, an abortive right-wing coup led by the army's commander-in-chief, widespread peasant disorders, and a renewed upswing in Bolshevik support and membership in the Petrograd Soviet, did Lenin decide to strike. Lev Trotsky had joined the Bolsheviks in August and was now chairman of both the Soviet and its Military Revolutionary Committee, which controlled the garrison's troops. On the night of 24–25 October platoons of armed workers, soldiers and sailors under the command of the Military Revolutionary Committee took over key installations in the capital. On the following night they attacked the Winter Palace and arrested the members of the last provisional government. The insurrection was later announced at a meeting of the second All-Russian Congress of Soviets, which was then in overnight session; and, following the withdrawal of Mensheviks and the peasant-based Socialist Revolutionary Party delegates, the now Bolshevik-dominated congress voted into office a new revolutionary government called the Council of People's Commissars, or *Sovnarkom*. Lenin was its chairman, and included in its initial membership with the brand new portfolio of nationalities policy was his loyal lieutenant, Joseph Stalin.

Four more years of bloody civil war were to elapse before the Red Army's victory over the counter-revolutionary Whites and the interventionist forces of their foreign backers finally established Soviet power throughout most of the old Russian Empire. Another year later, in 1922, Stalin was elected to the party office, which he would use to make that empire his own. But how was it that this little-known revolutionary from Georgia came to be appointed General Secretary of the All-Russian Communist Party (Bolsheviks)?

2

The underground revolutionary

Schooling

Lying just beyond the spectacular Caucasus Mountains on the broad isthmus between the Black Sea and the Caspian Sea, the ancient Orthodox Christian kingdom of Georgia had been absorbed into the Russian Empire in the late eighteenth and early nineteenth centuries. Russian tutelage was initially welcomed as it afforded the Georgian people a measure of protection from their traditional Muslim enemies, Persia and the Ottoman Empire. As the nineteenth century progressed, the Russian colonial administration introduced a process of gradual industrialization, economic modernization, education and urbanization that stimulated the growth of a vigorous nationalist movement among the Georgian intelligentsia. The fact that most native Georgians were at the bottom of the social heap, while Armenians and Russians dominated respectively the commercial middle classes and the governing bureaucracy, meant that nationalist sentiments were closely bound up with social divisions and class-consciousness. Socialism and nationalism were therefore natural allies in the struggle against the Russian imperial regime. For this reason many young Georgian radicals, as well as Jews and Poles, came to play a leading role in the all-Russian Marxist revolutionary movement in the early years of the twentieth century, and it was out of their ranks that Stalin was to emerge as one of the most powerful dictators of that century. His future eminence, however, was belied by his obscure origins.

He was born Iosif Vissarionovich Djugashvili on 9 December 1879 in the small town of Gori, about sixty kilometres west of the Georgian capital, Tiflis, now known as Tbilisi. He spent his infancy with his impoverished parents in a ramshackle hovel that also served as his shoemaker father's workshop. Many years later the place of his humble nativity was to be refurbished, immured within a magnificent, marble-colonnaded pavilion, and turned into a national shrine. Very little of any significance is known about his early childhood and it was therefore in all probability totally unremarkable. We know that he was a generally robust, intelligent and devout young boy, though short in stature and facially scarred by the pit-marks of an early smallpox attack. He was also slightly lame in his left arm, though sources vary as to the cause. His father was something of a drunkard and in 1884 he left his failed cobbler's business to find employment as a worker in a Tiflis shoe factory. Stalin could therefore claim both artisanal and proletarian parentage. Rather than following his father's footsteps into the shoe trade, little Joseph ('Soso') was very fortunate, as the child of near-paupers, to be enrolled at the local elementary school run by the Orthodox Church. By all accounts he was a bright, diligent pupil and eventually completed his course with sufficient distinction for his teachers to recommend his matriculation into the Tiflis Orthodox Theological Seminary, one of the foremost higher-educations institutions in the whole Transcaucasian region.

The move to the capital (in 1894) was to be a momentous step for the young Djugashvili. In the absence of any university in the area, the Tiflis Seminary attracted many of the most intelligent and independent-minded youth of Georgia into its austere surroundings, where a highly rigorous, if naturally heavily ecclesiastical, education was to be acquired. Tiflis was also then the centre of Georgian intellectual unrest, where narrow national dissidence jostled with a growing awareness of more cosmopolitan radical philosophies through the medium of the Russian language. As part of the St Petersburg government's heavy-handed campaign of 'Russification', restrictions on the use of native languages in the non-Russian borderlands and the compulsory use of Russian in many schools and official institutions were widespread. While the authorities hoped that this would result in a greater degree of cultural, intellectual and political conformity, it also had the unlooked-for consequence of making available to a wider readership not only the works of Russian authors, but also Russian translations of the artistic, scientific, secular and subversive literature of the West. Although such books were banned to the seminarists, it was through his illicit reading of proscribed texts from the city library that the future Stalin first came into conflict with the seminary authorities. A series of punishments failed to dampen his intellectual curiosity and served only to reinforce the spirit of rebelliousness and anti-authoritarianism now growing inside him. The combination of resentment at his personal treatment and the actual contents of the forbidden literature gradually caused him to question not only the authority of the monks and priests who taught him, but also the very religious principles on which their teaching was based. Exactly when Djugashvili abandoned his faith in Christianity is as unclear as the precise timing of his espousal of revolutionary Marxism as his new, alternative orthodoxy, but it was certainly some time during his five years at the Tiflis Seminary, from which he was duly expelled in May 1899.

The official reason for his expulsion was *not* the dissemination of Marxist propaganda, as he was later to maintain; but obviously his deteriorating conduct and academic performance were not unlinked to his increasing involvement in illegal political activities among the capital's radical intelligentsia and working class. His experience at the seminary was not, however, wasted. Throughout his life the former theological seminarist can be detected in his rigid dogmatism, his rhetorical and literary style, his capacity for diligent and repetitive work, and also in his duplicity and deceitfulness – first developed in his relations with the seminary authorities and later to became one of the hallmarks of his political style. So Djugashvili's formal education was now over; his political education in the revolutionary underground was just about to begin.

Struggle

In 1898 the first, founding congress of the Marxist Russian Social Democratic Workers' Party was held in the town of Minsk in Belorussia. Only a handful of delegates attended and it achieved almost nothing in concrete results. It was, however, one of the first, hesitant steps of the infant party, which was soon to grow into such a potent force in Russian history. In the same year Djugashvili joined a small social-democratic organization in Tiflis called *Messame Dassy* ('The Third Group'). Of course the 19-year-old seminary student had only a rudimentary knowledge of Marxist philosophy, and his receptiveness to socialism was the result more of an instinctive awareness and practical experience of the Georgian workers' grievances than of an intellectual understanding of political and economic theory. In the words of one of his biographers, 'his socialism was cold, sober and rough', and stemmed not from sentiment, moral indignation or book-learning, but from the personal circumstances of his boyhood and youth among the disadvantaged and exploited lower classes of Georgian society. It came therefore not from the heart or the mind, but from the gut.

Although he had previously frequented radical discussion circles, membership of The Third Group gave the future Stalin his first experience of practical propaganda work among the Tiflis proletariat. As this would certainly bring him to the attention of the police, he needed to adopt a pseudonym and so chose the name of a Georgian romantic literary hero, 'Koba'. This was the first of many aliases he assumed before the name Stalin (from the Russian word for steel – *stal*') finally stuck. For the next two or three years Koba/Djugashvili was active in propaganda, agitational and organizational work both in Tiflis and in the Black Sea coastal town of Batumi, always taking a hard, militant line in any theoretical or practical disputes with his comrades and simultaneously deepening his understanding of the ideological dimensions of the struggle. In 1902 he was arrested, imprisoned and exiled to eastern Siberia, from where he escaped and made his way back to Georgia in 1904.

During his absence the second congress of the RSDRP had taken place, at which the fateful split between the Bolsheviks and the Mensheviks occurred. Koba was probably unfamiliar with the niceties of the dispute which had caused the division, but temperamentally and intuitively he was more inclined to the Bolshevik camp, unlike the majority of the more moderate Georgian social democrats, many of whom, like N. S. Chkheidze (1864–1926) and I. G. Tsereteli (1881–1960), later became prominent among the leadership of the Mensheviks. The fact that the Bolshevik social democrats were in a minority in Transcaucasia meant that the somewhat abrasive and individualistic Koba acquired a high profile among them and soon came to the attention of the party's national leadership.

The first meeting between Lenin and Stalin took place at a party conference in Finland in December 1905, though there is no evidence that the young Georgian activist made any great impression on the Bolshevik leader. In the following year a so-called 'unification congress' of the party's Menshevik and Bolshevik factions convened in Stockholm, and once more Koba made the journey north, the first time the 26-year-old had set foot outside the Russian Empire.

Here, too, he made his maiden speech to a party congress, asserting his individualism by criticizing both the Menshevik and Bolshevik positions on the agrarian question, but otherwise toeing a strictly Leninist line. In the spring of 1907 he once again attended the party congress, this time in London, and although he took no active part in the proceedings his repeated presence among Lenin's supporters at these meetings was beginning to establish him as an apparently consistent and reliable opponent of Menshevism, which was more than could be said for the maverick Lev Trotsky. Stalin would later contrast his own early loyalty to the Bolshevik cause with Trotsky's theoretical disputes with Lenin, to great political advantage.

Needless to say, neither the 1906 nor the 1907 congress succeeded in forging the reunification of the two factions, and they continued to be divided on a whole range of internal ideological and organizational issues that consumed much time and energy over the ensuing decade. Apart from the fundamental differences over the role of the party and the strategy of revolution, there were two particularly contentious problems over which there could be no agreement. One was the so-called 'liquidator' debate. The question was whether, now that the revolutionary events of 1905 had created a more liberal political climate with free elections to the State Duma and legal political parties, there was any longer any need to maintain a clandestine revolutionary underground organization or, on the contrary, it could be 'liquidated' – that is, dismantled. Most Mensheviks favoured its liquidation, while Lenin and the Bolsheviks insisted that the undercover network of agents and their covert operations be maintained. The second issue concerned the question of 'expropriations'. This was the euphemism used to describe the policy of acquiring party funds by means of illicit, even criminal, activities, including the robbing of state banks. As on the liquidator matter, the Mensheviks preferred to operate entirely within the legal framework, whereas the less scrupulous Bolsheviks considered it quite legitimate in the revolutionary cause to expropriate by all available means funds which they believed had in any case been expropriated from the toiling masses in the first place. Consequently, the Bolsheviks continued to enjoy the proceeds of the strong-arm tactics of their 'fighting squads'. The expropriation campaign affected Stalin in particular as the Caucasus, with its mountainous terrain and long tradition of brigandage, was a favourite region for acts of violent revolutionary banditry. One of the most notorious exploits was a brazen and bloodthirsty attack on a coachful of money bound for the Tiflis State Bank in June 1907, which resulted in several killings and a haul of over 300,000 rubles. The raid was led by an old comrade of Stalin, a flamboyant Armenian terrorist known as 'Kamo' Ter Petrossian; and although it is unlikely that Stalin himself had any direct hand in the robbery, intensified police activity in Tiflis following the incident possibly influenced his decision to shift his operational base from Tiflis to the centre of the Russian oil industry, Baku, on the shores of the Caspian Sea.

The police in Baku, however, were no less vigilant than elsewhere, and in March 1908 Koba was once more arrested and sent for another spell of internal exile from which he escaped even more easily than the first time and returned to Baku. He was soon re-arrested and escorted back to complete his sentence. On his release in 1911 he decided to move to St Petersburg but was promptly expelled from the capital. (The fairly lenient sentences that Stalin received, and the ease with which he so often escaped, have led some biographers to suggest that he may have been on the police payroll as an informant. Although there were indeed many such double agents at the time, there is no concrete evidence that Djugashvili/Koba/Stalin was one of them.) In the next year he was appointed a member of the Bolshevik Central Committee following the 'Bolsheviks-only' party congress in Prague at which the divorce between Lenin's party and the Mensheviks became absolute. Despite later attempts at reconciliation, the Bolsheviks and Mensheviks were now effectually two separate parties, with separate policies and separate organizations. His elevation to the party leadership was no doubt a reward for the uncompromisingly anti-Menshevik line pursued by Stalin, as he now came invariably to be called. At about the same time he also joined the editorial board of the party newspaper, *Pravda*, on which he continued to argue forcefully against those who still retained hopes of a Menshevik–Bolshevik reconciliation. After another brush with the law and yet another escape from Siberian exile, Stalin was now entrusted by Lenin with a major piece of theoretical writing. This was a long essay on 'Marxism and the National Problem', which was published in 1913 and firmly established the Georgian Bolshevik as the party's leading theoretician on the relationship between class, nationalism and the revolution.

Like other leading Bolsheviks, however, he was not around to witness or participate in the actual revolution, which broke out in February 1917. In February 1913 the police had caught up with him yet again and this time decided to banish him to a remote spot in northern Siberia beyond the Arctic Circle. Although he was later allowed to reside further south, he remained in his desolate Siberian exile until the authority of the tsarist police who expelled him collapsed in the ruins of the regime they served.

1917

Like hundreds of other political victims of the Siberian exile system, Stalin immediately seized the opportunity presented by the February Revolution to return as quickly as possible to European Russia and join in the fray. When he arrived in Petrograd on 12 March the political situation was understandably complex and confused. In addition to the confrontational alliance between the Provisional Government and the Soviet (i.e. 'dual power'), the unexpected abdication of the tsar had thrown up a number of urgent issues which exercised all the parties of the left. The most pressing of these were the question of Russia's continuing participation in the war; the possibility of bringing about the reunification of the RSDRP; and the problem of how much support should be given by the socialists to the bourgeois Provisional Government. Initially, the Bolshevik newspaper, *Pravda*, which was being run by three fairly junior party activists, adopted a basically tough attitude on all three questions. However, with the arrival of Stalin and another senior member of the party's Central Committee, G. E. Zinoviev (1883–1936), the editorial line shifted to a more conciliatory position which reflected the generally held assumption in the party that the revolution would not swiftly transcend the limits of bourgeois democracy. Stalin's personal position was somewhat equivocal: while rejecting the hard-left line, he did not go so far as to embrace the policy either of 'revolutionary defencism' (i.e. continuing to fight imperial Germany) or of political collaboration with the Mensheviks and the Provisional Government. Whether this was owing to lack of conviction or to political calculation is difficult to determine.

Even after Lenin's return and the enunciation of the *April Theses*, Stalin did not immediately throw his weight behind the startling new initiative, but before very long force of circumstances made him Lenin's virtual spokesman in the capital. The decisive factor promoting Stalin to his new eminence within the party was the decision of the Provisional Government's new Prime Minister, Alexander Kerensky (1881–1970), to arrest the Bolshevik leaders, including Lenin, in the aftermath of violent demonstrations in July that greeted yet another Russian military débâcle at the front. In the event Lenin decided not to submit to arrest, and instead went into hiding across the Finnish border. However, he and several other prominent Bolsheviks who *were* arrested, as well as Trotsky who had recently declared his solidarity with them, were now temporarily *hors de combat*, and in their absence Stalin thereby acquired a new authority. He was now not only a member of the Central Committee; he was also still a deputy on the Petrograd Soviet and editor of the party's newspaper (renamed *Rabochii Put'* – 'The Workers' Road'). Lacking the flamboyance, charisma or erudition of the Bolsheviks' intellectual elite, Stalin nevertheless played a vital role during the next few weeks in the day-to-day routine work of organizing committees, cadres and caucuses, as well as editing *Rabochii Put'* and generally keeping things going at a time when party fortunes were at a low ebb.

It is impossible to say whether this led to any resentment on Stalin's part when Trotsky was released from gaol and began to overshadow him both as Chairman of the Petrograd Soviet and as a central figure in the planning and execution of the October Revolution. However, both of these roles were written out of the historical record during the period of Stalin's later ascendancy and Trotsky's political disgrace. Instead, a spurious version of the 'Great October Proletarian Socialist Revolution' was concocted that portrayed Stalin in the glorious role of Lenin's closest comrade-in-arms and veritable genius of the Revolution. On the other hand, attempts after Stalin's own death to belittle his role erred in the opposite direction. True, he kept a fairly low profile and held no operational command during the armed insurrection which overthrew the Provisional Government and declared 'All Power to the Soviets', but a recent western biographer suggests that there was really 'not a lot for him to do in the actual take-over' and that the same criticism, if criticism is called for, could be levelled at other prominent names in the party hierarchy. On the other hand, it is interesting to note that the famous eyewitness account of the Revolution written by the American journalist John Reed, *Ten Days that Shook the World*, contains not a single reference to Stalin, which no doubt accounts for the fact that the book was banned by Stalin in the 1930s and people found in possession of it were executed.

In the final analysis, it is not really important what Stalin actually did or where he actually was on the night of the insurrection. More important was the fact that despite his many years spent in the provinces, in prison or in exile, and despite his occasional minor differences with Lenin, he was sufficiently close to the centre of the action throughout the political turmoil of 1917, sufficiently well entrenched among the triumphant party's leading personnel, and sufficiently well experienced in organizational and ideological matters to win an automatic place as a People's Commissar (i.e. Minister) in Lenin's new revolutionary cabinet, the *Sovnarkom*. An added distinction was the fact that, of the fourteen commissariats created, Stalin's – the Commissariat for Nationalities – was the only one without a precedent in the pre-revolutionary administration of the tsars or Provisional Governments. The importance of the new office was soon to be demonstrated as the centrifugal forces of national independence threatened to dismember the fledgling revolutionary republic during the coming years of fratricidal civil war.

19

3

The General Secretary

Civil war

Sovnarkom's first two legislative acts were the Decree on Peace and the Decree on Land, published on 26 October 1917. Although the decrees notionally redeemed two of the Bolsheviks' revolutionary pledges – to secure peace for the country and land for the peasants – it was still the military situation and the agrarian crisis that were to prove the most intractable problems for the new regime over the next four difficult years. The most pressing task was to secure a separate peace with Germany. Trotsky, as Commissar for Foreign Affairs, was in charge of the Soviet negotiating team, but Stalin remained close to Lenin in Petrograd while the talks proceeded at Brest-Litovsk on the Russo-Polish frontier.

The issue of Russia's continuing participation in, or unilateral withdrawal from, the war with Germany had divided the Social Democrats ever since the commencement of hostilities in 1914. On the one hand were the so-called 'revolutionary defencists' who argued that they should support the war effort against imperialist Germany and, following an allied victory, only then concentrate on the revolutionary struggle at home. The 'revolutionary defeatists', however, urged the case that the national turmoil that would follow a Russian defeat would create a revolutionary situation and bring about the collapse of tsarism. Lenin was of neither camp, and advocated the transformation of the international war into a series of national revolutionary wars, the armed workers and peasants of each belligerent country turning their weapons from each other and training them on the 'bourgeois imperialist' governments of Europe. Lenin's determinedly internationalist stand at this point was a far cry from Stalin's later policy of building 'Socialism in One Country'.

After the October Revolution, the problem took on an extra dimension: it was not now a question of whether to fight and defend Russia against Germany, but whether to defend the home of the world's first proletarian socialist revolution against the Hohenzollern Empire. Those who argued for the latter course, led by Nikolai Bukharin (1888–1938), were chided by Lenin and dubbed the 'left Communists' who had no real grasp of the military situation. While Trotsky for his part pursued an ambiguous policy of 'neither peace, nor war', Lenin insisted that, with the German armies advancing ever closer to Petrograd, a separate peace must be secured at almost any cost.

Finally, the swingeing German peace terms were agreed to, with heavy losses in territory and economic resources on the Soviet side, which caused bitter misgivings and renewed divisions within the party leadership. Although Lenin and Stalin did not always see eye-to-eye on every detail of the Brest-Litovsk treaty negotiations, nevertheless the latter ultimately supported Lenin in his pragmatic policy of 'sacrificing space in order to gain time'. Time was indeed essential, for no sooner had the Soviet government withdrawn from the international conflict than it was faced with the military resistance of its political enemies at home, supported logistically, financially and militarily by the governments of the western capitalist powers who wished, not only to get Russia back into the war, but also, in Winston Churchill's words, 'to strangle bolshevism in its cradle'.

This is not the place to review the course of the savage hostilities that finally led to the Red Army's victory in the Russian Civil War. Over the next four years, the country was ripped apart during a brutal, nationwide conflict that raged from the Baltic to the Pacific and in which rivers of blood were spilt. From the Ukranian steppes, through the vast, frozen wastes of Siberia, pro-Bolshevik forces (the 'Reds'), counter-revolutionary armies (the 'Whites'), peasant guerrilla bands (the 'Greens'), ethnic minority movements, local war-lords and foreign interventionists engaged one another in campaigns of fratricidal slaughter. Amidst this military mayhem, the new Soviet government sought to consolidate its political authority over the country and introduce (in the areas which it controlled) the basis of an ideologically motivated, centralized, socialist economy called 'War Communism'.

There are many factors which help to explain the eventual Red triumph: Bolshevik control of the centre; access to First World War ammunition dumps; the political disunity of the White generals; withdrawal of the allied interventionist forces; and generally greater popular support for the revolutionary cause over those who would restore the old oppressive order. But some of the credit for the victory, albeit a pyrrhic victory, must also go to the creator of the Red Army, Lev Trotsky, though one would search in vain for any such acknowledgement in later official Soviet accounts of the conflict. The conditions of warfare also gave ample scope for Stalin to demonstrate not only his organizational and administrative skills, but also those personal attributes of ruthlessness, implacability and authoritarianism that he was to display throughout his entire career. Although he never had any soldier's training, he seemed at home in a military-style environment and was later to adopt regimental attitudes, titles and attire. Perhaps the greatest moment of his whole career was when he led the nation to victory over Nazi Germany in 1945. He was soon after to style himself as 'Generalissimo'.

During the Civil War he was active on a number of different military assignments and showed great energy shuttling back and forth between Moscow (now the capital) and the different fronts – the Baltic, Belorussia, Ukraine, Poland and the lower Volga – where his acerbic and overweening personality often brought him into conflicts of jurisdiction and authority with local military commanders. This, however, was a common phenomenon under the system of 'dual command' introduced into the Red Army by Trotsky, whereby military commanders, often ex-tsarist officers, were 'shadowed' by a party commissar to ensure the political reliability of their orders and operations.

An early and notorious example of this in Stalin's case was the 'Tsaritsyn affair' in 1918. Stalin was dispatched to the Volga town, which was later to bear his name, on a special mission to ensure the delivery of essential food supplies from the grain-growing areas to the north, which had been cut off by White forces. It was essentially a civilian assignment, but Stalin soon insisted on assuming plenipotentiary military powers in the region, which brought him into collision not only with the supreme commander of the southern front, but also, more ominously for their future relations, with the People's Commissar for War, Trotsky. Eventually, some kind of compromise was found, food supplies were maintained, the local White forces retreated, and Stalin was recalled to Moscow. Some authors have maintained that the Tsaritsyn affair was a crucial element in the deadly Stalin–Trotsky rivalry of later years. Be that as it may, it certainly did nothing to sweeten their relationship, and it encouraged in Stalin his taste for power, a contempt for so-called 'experts', and an unhealthy tendency to eliminate obstacles and opponents by the use of physical force.

In 1920, Stalin asked to be relieved of his military duties to devote more time and attention to the business of the Commissariat for Nationalities. During the Civil War there was only limited scope for him to exercise his powers in that post, as many non-Russian regions of the old empire were outside the direct control of Moscow. Many of the ethnic minority peoples had taken advantage of the chaos of revolution and civil war to further their struggle for national liberation and self-determination. This was, after all, in accordance with Bolshevik nationalities policy, so forcefully enunciated earlier by Stalin in his *Marxism and the National Problem* of 1913. Independence had in fact been attained by Finland, Poland and the Baltic states (Estonia, Latvia and Lithuania), but the Soviet government looked on with some alarm as more and more regions and peoples from Vilnius to Vladivostok sought to assert their independence from the centre. National liberation from the Russian Empire was one thing; secession from the Soviet Socialist Republic was quite another. In this respect, therefore, the Civil War was fought both to achieve the political cohesiveness and to maintain the territorial integrity of the young socialist state. The Commissar for Nationalities adopted a strictly centralist stand on this issue and strove determinedly to prevent the defection of would-be secessionist states and to regather under Moscow's wing those which had managed to establish some kind of quasi-autonomy, such as Ukraine.

In his native Transcaucasia, Stalin took a particularly hard line with the Menshevik-dominated independent government of Georgia. By 1920, neighbouring Armenia and Azerbaijan had been brought back into the Soviet fold, and in 1921, despite some initial misgivings by Lenin, the flower of Georgian independence was brutally nipped in the bud by Red Army troops. Denied even the status of a full Union Republic, the country was forcibly amalgamated with the newly established Transcaucasian Soviet Socialist Republic and later included in the Union of Soviet Socialist Republics (USSR), which was formally constituted in 1922. Not until 1936 was a semblance of statehood achieved, with the formation of the Georgian Soviet Socialist Republic.

As well as his responsibilities in government, by the time the Civil War was over Stalin had already accumulated a remarkable amount of bureaucratic power in his own hands. Despite some tactical mistakes and errors of political judgement, he had made a significant contribution to the Red Army victory which greatly enhanced his personal reputation within the party (renamed the 'All-Russian Communist Party (Bolsheviks)' in 1919). Although less in the limelight than some other prominent Bolsheviks, he had managed to establish himself as a crucial cog in the government and party apparatus (*apparat*) through his willingness to undertake a whole range of essential, though unglamorous and unheroic, duties and functions, which were possibly unattractive to his more sophisticated colleagues in the Kremlin leadership. Apart from the Commissariat for Nationalities, Stalin also headed the Workers' and Peasants' Inspectorate (*Rabkrin*) and was a member of the party's Organizational Bureau (*Orgburo*) and its powerful Political Bureau (*Politburo*). Each of these positions, by itself, gave him significant administrative and even executive power within the respective organizations. But combined in the hands of one man – a single-minded and manipulative man at that – that power became enormous. While his colleagues were engaged with more high-profile affairs, Stalin had succeeded unobtrusively to accumulate more bureaucratic authority than any other government or party official in the country. As if this were not enough, in April 1922 he was appointed to a newly created post which he was later to use as the springboard for his later dictatorial power – that of General Secretary of the Communist Party. Throughout the history of the Soviet Union, it was that post of *Gensec* of the CPSU, rather than that of Prime Minister or Head of State, that Stalin transformed into the paramount political position in the land. The new post was unremarkable in itself, and at the time of its creation was regarded simply as yet another administrative office in the ever-expanding bureaucratic machinery. If the seemingly lacklustre Georgian was prepared to undertake more routine duties and managerial chores, then his comrades in the party leadership appeared content to let him get on with it. Not even Trotsky, as far as we know, expressed any qualms at the time. One of the *Gensec*'s major functions was to prevent factionalism inside the Party, in keeping with Lenin's 'Resolution on Party Unity', adopted at the 10th Party Congress in 1921, which gave him the opportunity to control personnel, and hence enormous powers of patronage. However, by the time the significance of Stalin's role in his new office was fully realized, it was too late to prevent him from using it for his own ends.

NEP

The end of the Civil War did not mean that Soviet power was secure. After seven years' uninterrupted international, revolutionary and civil warfare, Lenin's government was now beset by a wave of peasant rebellion, by military and naval mutiny, industrial chaos, depopulation, famine, international ostracism and a desperate shortage of expert technical, cultural and managerial personnel. In particular, the economic dislocation caused by the highly centralized wartime policies known as 'War Communism' had antagonized the Russian peasantry to such an extent that Lenin was forced to reconsider his position and consolidate his power on a new foundation. In 1921 the hated grain-requisitioning squads of War Communism were abolished and replaced with a limited market economy in the countryside, which encouraged private enterprise and profit-making in an attempt to re-harness the cooperation of the peasantry. This was the first stage of Lenin's New Economic Policy (NEP).

NEP aroused bitter controversy within the party. Although the state still controlled heavy industry and had a monopoly on foreign trade – 'the commanding heights of the economy', in Lenin's phrase – agriculture, light manufacturing and the service industries were for the most part privately owned and managed, often by their previous owners. Many communists regarded this situation not simply as a strategic retreat from full-blown socialism and centralized planning, but at best as a compromise with capitalism and the class enemy, the bourgeoisie and the rich peasants (*kulaks*), which was insupportable during the era of what was supposed to be 'the dictatorship of the proletariat'. Some called it an 'economic Brest-Litovsk'. Lenin, however, argued that NEP was only a temporary measure, a tactical withdrawal that was essential for the stabilization of the economy, an increase in food production and the gradual reconstruction of industry. Everyone agreed that these things were necessary for the building of socialism, especially now that proletarian revolutions had failed to materialize elsewhere in Europe, but a fierce debate raged over how the desired objective should be achieved. Nikolai Bukharin, one of the party's ablest economic theorists, openly called on the Russian peasants to 'Get rich', while Trotsky and the left-wing economist, Preobrazhensky, argued that the peasant must be made to pay for industrialization and socialist construction through a process of 'primary socialist accumulation' – that is, squeezing capital out of the peasantry through a policy of increased taxation and agricultural pricing mechanisms. Workers' leaders complained that the initials NEP stood in reality for the 'New Exploitation of the Proletariat'.

The 'industrialization debate' was matched by another theoretical controversy over the right road to socialism, in which the two chief protagonists were Trotsky and Stalin. As early as 1906 Trotsky had formulated what came to be called his 'Theory of Permanent Revolution', in which he argued that the weakness of the Russian bourgeoisie meant that the leading role in the bourgeois-democratic revolution would be played by the proletariat, and that this would of necessity bring about the immediate transformation of the revolution into its proletarian stage and the establishment of socialism. In its turn the workers' revolution in Russia would act as the signal for a series of socialist revolutions in the advanced capitalist countries that would ensure that the Russian proletarian state would not be forced to maintain itself for long in political isolation.

Although Trotsky found many critics of his theory, including Lenin, the events of 1917 in Russia came very close to the first part of Trotsky's formulation. During the mid-twenties, however, as it became clear that the expected proletarian revolutions in the West were *not* about to take place, the question arose about the self-sufficiency of the Russian Revolution. In other words, was it possible, in the absence of world revolution, to build 'Socialism in One Country'? In a series of lectures delivered in 1924 entitled *Foundations of Leninism*, Stalin stated emphatically that the theory of permanent revolution was now untenable. Of course, he conceded, the 'final victory' of international socialism required 'the efforts of the proletarians in several advanced countries', but 'the uneven and spasmodic character of the development of the various capitalist countries . . . leads not only to the possibility, but also to the necessity of the victory of the proletariat *in individual countries*' [emphasis added]. In practical political terms, Stalin's policy of constructing socialism in one country was simply more attractive to the party rank-and-file and those in the population who understood such things than the prospect held out by Trotsky and others of further revolutionary struggle. Stalin's formula was in a sense an appeal to basic nationalist instincts rather than internationalist dogma. Intellectuals in the party like Trotsky and Zinoviev, the latter chairman of the Communist International organization (*Comintern*), were easily accused of lack of faith in the Russian Revolution and of a doctrinaire refusal to believe that the Soviet Union could 'go it alone' without the support of revolutions abroad. Their objections to Socialism in One Country, based on Marx's vision of world revolution, were, however, in the words of an American historian, 'ideologically impeccable and politically disastrous', particularly in the leadership struggle that followed Lenin's death in 1924.

That these economic debates and doctrinal disputes took place at all was of course a measure of the relative intellectual and political pluralism that existed during the 1920s in comparison with the rigid monolithism of the 'thirties. True, the country was already a one-party state and the activities of the political police (the *Cheka*, set up as early as December 1917) had eliminated all organized opposition to the Communists' monopoly of power. Within the party itself, the policy of 'democratic centralism' had been reinforced by the adoption of Lenin's 'Resolution on Party Unity' at the 10th Party Congress in 1921, which outlawed the existence of organized 'factions' within the party. Nevertheless, debate and discussion did take place, both inside and outside the party, on a scale and with a diversity that was not equalled until the late 1980s. It was a truly revolutionary, experimental era. NEP was itself an experiment, the first peacetime attempt at running a 'mixed economy' with both nationalized and private sectors peacefully co-existing. Entrepreneurship flourished. Private traders, prosperous peasants, 'bourgeois specialists' (*spetsy*), black marketeers and commodity dealers (the so-called *Nepmen*) plied their profitable businesses while the planners and politicians were locked in hot debate.

A cultural revolution, too, was taking place. Art and literature were in the avant-garde of contemporary European movements. Historians argued; critics contended; different schools of prose, poetry and the plastic arts vied for public attention as futurism, symbolism, imaginism, constructivism, formalism, realism and satire were challenged by the exponents of a self-consciously 'proletarian culture' (*Proletkult*). A whole constellation of innovative writers, artists, sculptors, dramatists, interior designers, cinematographers and scientists combined to make the 1920s one of the most vibrant, pulsating decades in the history of Russian culture. There was, too, a genuine attempt to make all this available to the masses. This involved such initiatives as a nationwide campaign to eradicate illiteracy, progressive educational experiments, the emancipation of women, easy availability of divorce and abortion, the establishment of 'workers faculties' (*rabfaks*) at the universities, the invention of new scripts for ethnic groups with no written language, and a reform of the Cyrillic alphabet, which simplified orthography and facilitated the printing of books and newspapers. In the clubs and bars of Moscow and Petrograd, the 'fox-trot' was all the rage.

To describe the 1920s as 'the halcyon days of the revolution', as one recent popular history has it, is to embroider reality. Alongside the relative freedoms and enthusiasms, the arguments and experimentation of the NEP period, there were also the evils of famine, poverty, unemployment, censorship, an oppressive bureaucracy and all the coercive paraphernalia of an embryonic police state. But if one should not idealize the 1920s, neither should one necessarily regard them as the thin end of a Stalinist totalitarian wedge. However, as the decade drew to a close, NEP – Lenin's controversial 'compromise with capitalism' – was abandoned and Stalin began to put into drastic effect his own authoritarian version of Socialism in One Country.

Power

Before studying Stalin's 'revolution from above', it is first necessary to examine how his appointment as General Secretary in 1922 enabled him to emerge as virtual dictator in 1928. Even before Lenin's death in January 1924, the other members of the party Politburo were manoeuvring for position in the struggle for the leadership succession. In actual fact there was no formal office of 'party leader', but Lenin, who understood the realities of power politics, already realized as he lay terminally ill how the probable battle lines were being drawn. Although the Revolution had been won under the slogan of 'All Power to the Soviets', real power during the Civil War period had become more and more concentrated in the hands of the Bolshevik Party. Willy-nilly, the organs of central and local government, the soviets, had to rely to some extent on the services and expertise of functionaries and office-holders inherited from the old regime, whose political reliability was naturally suspect. In response, the party began to develop its own parallel bureaucracy or *apparat* at both central and provincial levels in which full-time party officials (*cadres*) gradually dominated the administration of government as well as party policy. For the most part these new professional party bureaucrats (*apparatchiki*) were drawn from the most radical and active ranks of the working class, still fired by class hatred of the surviving representatives of the old regime, to some extent suspicious of intellectuals and 'experts', and filled with a sometimes coarse enthusiasm for the 'dictatorship of the proletariat'. However, a combination of death in war, de-urbanization and dislocation of industry, unemployment and recruitment into the party hierarchy created a situation in which, to use Isaac Deutscher's phrase, by 1921 the Bolsheviks were in the position of a 'revolutionary élite without a revolutionary class behind it'. Given the class origins of the young *apparatchiki*, the result was not so much the dictatorship of the proletariat as a 'dictatorship of some former proletarians'. This, as the young Trotsky had prophesied much earlier in the century, would inevitably develop, or deteriorate, into the dictatorship of one man. It was not long before that prophecy was to become grim reality.

It soon became clear that the body which dominated and controlled the newly emerging party bureaucracy was in a position of enormous power and influence. That body was the party Secretariat. Whoever dominated the Secretariat wielded commensurate authority. After 1922 that man was Joseph Stalin. From his office the General Secretary was able to issue administrative directives, organize agenda, make appointments, recommend promotion and dismissals, distribute personnel, and shuffle the cadres in accordance with his own preferences and ambitions. By the time Lenin died, therefore, Stalin had built up a formidable power base within the party apparatus from which he could with relative ease and on plausible pretexts conveniently isolate or neutralize those who stood in his way.

Lenin suffered his first stroke in 1922, and now, from his sickbed, the invalided revolutionary leader warned of the dangers of such a huge concentration of bureaucratic power in Stalin's grip. In 1922 he composed a memorandum for the guidance of the Central Committee, later known as his 'Testament', in which he evaluated the political and personal qualities of the members of the Politburo. All came in for a fair amount of criticism, but only in Stalin's case did the dying leader recommend removal from office. 'Comrade Stalin', it read, 'having become General Secretary, has unlimited authority concentrated in his hands, and I am not sure whether he will always be capable of using that authority with sufficient caution'. A few days later he added: 'Stalin is too rude, and this defect . . . is intolerable in a General Secretary. That is why I suggest that the comrades think about a way to remove Stalin from that post'. In his place they should appoint someone who is 'more tolerant, more loyal, more courteous and more considerate of the comrades, less capricious etc.'. The arrogant, ill-mannered, 'nasty' side of Stalin's personality,', to which there are many testimonies, fleetingly threatened his political career. However, although the details of the Testament were announced to the 1924 Party Congress, Lenin's posthumous warning was ignored and Stalin was confirmed in office by a congress that was already packed with men who owed their positions to the patronage of the General Secretary.

Stalin also survived the shifting alliances within the Politburo. At first an informal 'triumvirate' of Stalin, Zinoviev and L. B. Kamenev (1883–1936) was formed to prevent Trotsky from taking over Lenin's mantle. The party leadership was well aware of the dangers of 'Bonapartism' – that is, the emergence of a military dictator out of the flames of revolution – and Trotsky appeared to be the obvious candidate. However, by the time Zinoviev and Kamenev realized that the threat came from elsewhere, they had already compromised themselves too much to do anything effective about it. Given their previous opposition to Trotsky, the new anti-Stalin alliance of Trotsky, Zinoviev and Kamenev, was easy to denigrate as opportunist, anti-party and, following on the 1921 'Resolution on Party Unity', factionalist. The penalty for factionalism was expulsion, and in 1927, during the tenth-anniversary year of the Revolution, all three Bolshevik leaders were expelled from the party. Zinoviev and Kamenev later recanted their errors and were temporarily readmitted to membership. Trotsky, on the other hand, was finally banished from the Soviet Union altogether in 1929, thus beginning his long decade of exile and tireless, bitter denunciations of Stalin's 'betrayal' of the Revolution.

Although intellectually Trotsky's inferior, Stalin was by far the cleverer politician. He had out-manoeuvred his arch-rival on every possible front, not least through his skilful manipulation of the 'cult' of Leninism which was established immediately after the Bolshevik leader's death and in which Stalin, the ex-seminarist, appeared in the role of high priest. In death Lenin was immortalized, almost deified, and a whole idolatrous cult built around his name, with all the ritual trappings, ceremonial, sacred texts and symbols, mythology and hagiography of a major religion. Lenin the atheist, humanist and materialist would have turned in his grave, if he had been granted the dignity of having one. Instead, his body was artificially preserved, mummified and placed on public display, where it still remains in its mausoleum, until recently the focal point of the nation's secular worship.

Like any self-respecting religion, the cult of Leninism also had its early heretics and apostates. Having successfully excommunicated them, Stalin now proceeded to lead the Soviet people into the promised land of Socialism in One Country. The exhilaration and energy of the revolutionary years and the comparatively vibrant variety of the 1920s was about to be replaced by the monochrome monolithism of the 'thirties. The methods employed in this process were to turn the country into a purgatory of human suffering and grief.

4

The totalitarian dictator

Collectivization

Although Stalin, no expert in economic theory, had not played a prominent role in the industrialization debate of the mid-twenties, he had never displayed particular affection for the peasantry and, despite personal animosities, leaned more towards those like Trotsky who favoured a programme of intensified industrialization at the peasants' expense. The rout of the so-called 'Left Opposition' (Trotsky, Zinoviev and company) in 1927 now gave Stalin a free hand to implement their economic policies without recognizing their contribution or granting them political favour. In 1928 he launched two major initiatives that were to plunge the country into an upheaval as great as the revolutions of 1917. These were the collectivization of agriculture and the first five-year plan for the rapid industrialization of the economy – Stalin's 'revolution from above'.

Despite a fair harvest in the autumn of 1927, by the winter the country faced an agricultural crisis. Against the background of an international war-scare when it was widely believed that the capitalist powers were planning another military intervention, the peasantry began to withhold grain from the market and hoard it in anticipation of higher prices being paid by government procurement agencies. Consequently, a number of government and party officials were dispatched to the provinces to investigate and report on the situation. Stalin personally travelled to the Urals and western Siberia. There he solved the problem with a characteristic lack of ceremony. Whereas other party stalwarts still tried to reason with the peasants and to operate within the constraints of the market and NEP, Stalin simply applied naked force. Having observed the situation on the ground, he set up road blocks to impede movement, ordered in military detachments and armed requisition squads, coercing the peasants to surrender their produce under threat of criminal prosecution for 'speculation' (outlawed under article 107 of the Soviet Criminal Code) or even grimmer consequences. It was a kind of reversion to the heavy-handed tactics of War Communism; but it worked. Grain procurements (i.e. confiscations) rose in volume, and Stalin determined to employ the 'Urals-Siberian method' on an even wider scale in an effort to destroy the economic power of the rich peasantry. This policy came to be sinisterly known as 'de-kulakization' – that is, the annihilation of the kulaks as a class. It should be noted at this point that the term 'kulak' (literally in Russian, a 'fist') was an extremely elastic one. If it was originally coined to designate a 'rich' peasant, then how rich was rich? And did they really constitute a 'class'? During the collectivization campaign, some frenzied local officials employed the definition with astonishing arbitrariness, often condemning peasants of modest means who sought to improve their income and life-styles as 'ideological kulaks'. They were to suffer the same fate as those more prosperous and successful agriculturists who had taken Bukharin's exhortation to 'Enrich yourselves!' at face value. The consequences were catastrophic.

Opposition to Stalin's strong-arm methods came not just from the peasants but from within the Politburo. A so-called 'Right Opposition' led by Bukharin and the head of the government, Aleksei Rykov, objected not only to Stalin's unilateral break with Lenin's conciliatory policy of accommodating the peasants, but also to his arrogant flouting of the Politburo's collective authority. However, very much alive to the dangers of 'factionalism', the Rightists failed to organize themselves into a coherent opposition movement and found little resonance to their objections within the party *apparat* or rank-and-file. In any case, the *apparat* was firmly under Stalin's control, and the short-lived Right Opposition soon followed the Left into the political wilderness. As Alec Nove has pointed out, this was:

> . . . a great turning point in Russian history. It upset once and
> for all the delicate psychological balance . . . between party
> and peasants . . . it was also the first time that a major policy

32

departure was undertaken by Stalin personally, without even the pretence of a central committee or politbureau decision.

From 1929 the collectivization drive proceeded – quite literally – in deadly earnest. The Russian countryside was once again turned into a battlefield as millions of peasant households, traditional communes, landholdings, livestock and equipment were commandeered at gunpoint and dragooned into the huge new party-controlled collective enterprises. Kulaks were exempted. Instead, their property was confiscated and they were rounded up, herded into cattle-wagons, and forcibly transported in their millions to the ice-bound wastelands of Siberia and the far north where they were either left to rot or else turned into convict labourers in the work camps and industrialization projects of the five-year plan. Many resisted collectivization by burning their crops, refusing to sow, or slaughtering their herds and flocks rather than surrendering them to the collective farm (kolkhoz). The results, not unnaturally, were disastrous; so much so that in the spring of 1930 Stalin called a temporary halt to the campaign. In an article entitled 'Dizzy with Success', which is breathtaking in its hypocrisy, he thundered against the misplaced zealotry of local officials who in an excess of enthusiasm had rushed the process of collectivization at a breakneck speed, recklessly distorting objectives, ignoring local conditions, skipping stages and – in a grotesque understatement – 'irritating the peasant collective farmer'!

After a temporary pause, the assault – for that is what it was – was resumed, and by 1932 over 60 per cent of all peasant households had joined the kolkhoz, in comparison to only around one per cent during the NEP. The calamitous consequences of the policy cannot be exaggerated. It yielded what has been described as a 'harvest of sorrow' for the Russian land. The collectivization drive was in effect a civil war unleashed by the party on the peasant population in which millions perished as a result of massacres, enforced deportations and man-made famines that decimated whole provinces. When delivery quotas were unfulfilled, Stalin questioned the loyalty and the efficiency of local party officials, who reacted with renewed savagery in exacting non-existent surpluses from starving peasant families. In Ukraine, a military cordon was thrown around the entire republic to prevent news of the mass starvation reaching the outside world. Millions perished in what had once been known as 'the breadbasket of Europe'. Only recently has the Russian government begun to admit the sheer scale of the tragedy and to acknowledge that other, less brutal, less devastating

33

options were available to bring about the transformation of the Soviet Union from an agrarian to a modern industrial society.

Like the rest of that society, collective farmers (*kolkhozniki*) were now mobilized to perform the bidding of the economic planners, delivering their compulsory quotas to the state at state-fixed prices, dependent on the government for mechanized equipment which was controlled through official Machine Tractor Stations (MTSs), tied to the land by a system of internal passports, and forced to respond to the dictates of party policy rather than the natural rhythms and requirements of the soil. Environmental conditions, irrigation and fertility patterns, seasonal fluctuations, local knowledge and custom were often ignored by city-trained agronomists whose scientific theories overruled traditional peasant wisdom and working cycles. Three-quarters of a century after the abolition of peasant bondage in Russia, the lot of the collective farmers in Stalin's USSR cannot have seemed so different from that of their enserfed forebears.

Another consequence of collectivization was the migration, part voluntary, part enforced, of nearly ten million able-bodied young peasants from the villages to join the new industrial armies of the first five-year plan (see below).

Industrialization

In both practical and ideological terms, 'building socialism' meant economic modernization and industrialization. None of the participants in the great debates of the 1920s had disagreed on that. The arguments were over means rather than ends. Having defeated the Left Opposition, in 1928 Stalin authorized the implementation of a complex programme setting out industrial targets for the Soviet Union's economic growth over the next quinquennium, which in its scale and ambition went far beyond the projects of the most critical opponents of NEP. This was the first of the famous 'five-year plans', which were the central feature of the Soviet 'command economy' thereafter. During the period of the plan – actually concluded, if not technically completed, in four years (1929–32) – the last remaining vestiges of small-time capitalism were abolished, the *Nepmen* were eliminated, private enterprises were renationalized, and a crash programme of heavy industrial development was forced through with all the aggressive intensity and militant enthusiasm of a military campaign. Indeed, the imagery and the vocabulary of war were constantly used to describe its various features. Party propaganda trumpeted of 'industrial fronts', 'shock troops', 'storming fortresses', creating 'bastions' and of rooting out the enemy in the shape of 'spies and saboteurs'. There was, in fact, a close and conscious correlation in Stalin's mind between industrial achievement and national security, underlined by the plan's heavy emphasis on those branches of the economy that were either geared, or could be turned, to military purpose and production. Stalin made this quite explicit in a much-quoted speech of 1931 in which he blamed Russia's economic backwardness for her long record of military beatings at the hands of

> Mongol khans, . . . Turkish beys, . . . French and British capitalists . . . and Japanese barons. . . . We are fifty or a hundred years behind the advanced countries. We must make good this distance in ten. Either we do it, or they will crush us.

To achieve this end the whole of Soviet society was mobilized and given its orders, tasks and often unrealizable targets to fulfil. Every sector, factory, workshop, bench and work brigade had its own allotted 'norm', its individual contribution to the plan. The whole apparatus of state control, propaganda and coercion swung into action to inspire, exhort or bully the nation on to ever more impossible endeavours. Huge new industrial complexes were erected in virgin territory; great dams and hydroelectric stations were built to harness the power of Russia's mighty rivers; while fuels, minerals and raw materials were torn from the permafrost by multitudes of convict labourers toiling in the remotest regions of Siberia. So-called 'shock workers' who overfulfilled their norm became national heroes, like Aleksei Stakhanov, the legendary miner of the mid-'thirties whose name became a byword for superhuman effort. Those who underfulfilled were subject to a draconian code of labour discipline which punished absenteeism, unpunctuality, inefficiency and sloth. Not all the targets were reached, but underproduction was blamed on class enemies, industrial saboteurs and the agents of foreign powers. Show trials were held of foreign experts and engineers working in Russia, accused of deliberate 'wrecking' and other criminal activities against the state and against socialism.

Despite shortfalls in certain sectors, in 1932 the plan was declared to have been fulfilled. A tremendous leap forward had been made in industrial output, particularly in the metallurgical industries. Socialist planning methods appeared to have been vindicated at a time when western capitalism seemed to be in ruins, racked by mass unemployment and economic depression. In material terms the achievements and triumphs of the early five-year plans were truly heroic. It is impossible to put even approximate figures on production levels, as the official statistics were, to say the least, untrustworthy, but there was no denying that the foundations had been well and truly laid for the transformation of the USSR into an industrial giant. In human terms, however, the cost of this industrial progress was staggering. Machinery and equipment had at first to be bought from abroad, purchased with the revenue from exports of grain screwed from the collective farmers while the people starved. Food and consumer goods disappeared from the shops; interminable queuing became a regular feature of daily existence; rationing was introduced; housing conditions in the overcrowded cities were appalling; wages failed to keep pace with rocketing prices. Under socialism, Stalin assured the Soviet people, 'life is getting better, more joyful'.

Life was certainly getting different. The economic transformation brought about by collectivization and industrialization was accompanied by a social and cultural revolution. Soviet society now consisted officially of two classes, the workers and the *kolkhozniki*, and a social 'stratum' of educated white-collar workers and professional personnel known as the 'intelligentsia'. Everyone, not just workers and peasants, had their part to play in the plan. Even creative writers were to be, in Stalin's phrase, 'engineers of human souls' and a new literary/political formula called 'Socialist Realism' was introduced as a yardstick against which all kinds of artistic endeavour were to be measured. Censorship controls were reinforced to ensure that authors wrote only in such a way as to enhance and glorify the victory of socialism. Gone were the independent literary groupings of the 1920s, replaced in 1934 by the Union of Soviet Writers, a kind of literary closed shop whose members assembled novels and stories full of compulsory optimism and positive heroes. Lyricism, romance, formalism and satire were taboo. Instead, the state-owned printing presses churned out the monochrome conveyor-belt novels of the five-year plan with such 'riveting' titles as Katayev's *Time, Forward!* (1932), Ostrovsky's *How the Steel was Tempered* (1935), and the reprint of Gladkov's *Cement*. Originally published in 1924, Gladkov's story about the opening of a cement factory after the Civil War set the tone for the later canonical works of Socialist Realism, most of which had little to do with socialism and still less with reality.

Not only literature, but all other forms of artistic, intellectual and even scientific activity were subject to ideological requirements. Stalin himself became the final arbiter on every academic discipline from agronomy to zoology. Biologists, geneticists, lawyers, linguists and musicians were forced to toe the party line. History became the handmaiden of the state. The great figures of Russia's past, temporarily debunked by the Marxist historiography of the 'twenties, were rehabilitated. Strong rulers like Alexander Nevsky, Ivan the Terrible and Peter the Great, military leaders like Generals Suvorov and Kutuzov, were now depicted as national heroes. The analogy with the wise and omnipotent Stalin was deliberate and unmistakable. On the other hand, heroes of the revolutionary struggle of 1917, Trotsky in particular, were ignominiously 'unpersoned' and cast into historical limbo. A recent book published in the West, entitled *The Commissar Vanishes*, records, with plenty of pictorial evidence, how even well-known photographs and official paintings were doctored by Stalin's censors to brush out or paint over representations of disgraced or condemned public figures. And, as recently as 2003, a distinguished professor of history at Moscow State University confided to this author that he and his generation 'don't know much about Trotsky'.

As the 'thirties wore on, other remnants of the past were revived in an attempt to replace the libertarianism of the revolutionary period with more order, discipline and control. Educational experiments were scrapped and schools made to reintroduce learning by rote, formal examinations, a core curriculum and school uniforms. In personal relationships, cohabitation, easy divorce and abortion on demand were all but abolished as the virtues of the stable nuclear family, fecundity and parenthood were stressed. 'Mother-heroines' who produced ten children or more were awarded medals by the grateful state, a reflection, perhaps, of the five-year plan's emphasis on quantitative achievement. In the armed services, there was a return to the use of tsarist ranks and titles for the officer class, together with more elaborate uniforms, insignia, epaulettes and other regalia. In civil society the concept of 'dangerous egalitarianism' was officially condemned and a whole range of wage and salary differentials, perks and privileges, special shops and exclusive honours introduced for members of what Milovan Djilas called 'the New Class' of party bosses and the bureaucratic establishment. Stalin's revolution from above had abandoned the pristine revolutionary slogans of 'Liberty, Equality, Fraternity' in favour of oppression, inequality and strife.

In 1934 the Party celebrated its successes at the 17th Congress – triumphantly entitled the 'Congress of Victors'. The worst excesses of collectivization and the first five-year plan were at an end; socialism had been achieved and the old class enemies defeated; the second five-year plan promised more to the consumer; old oppositionists had been (temporarily) readmitted to the party fold; soon a new constitution of the USSR was to be drafted, which was hailed as 'the most democratic in the world'. After the sacrifices, there was a sense of accomplishment and a mood of self-congratulation. The worst, it seemed, was over. But the worst was yet to come.

Terror

Just at the time when his power seemed more secure, when the Party seemed united, when the industrial and agricultural economies were showing results and the sacrifices of the recent past seemed justified, Stalin plunged the entire country into a paroxysm of pain and sheer terror that many still believe to be unprecedented in human history.

The first target of his attack was the Party itself, and the first victim was the popular leader of the Leningrad party organization, Sergei Kirov (1886–1934). Kirov was shot at his headquarters on 1 December 1934 by an ex-member of the Communist Youth Organization named Leonid Nikolayev. Although it has never been definitely proven, and it is still a controversial topic, there is much circumstantial evidence to suggest that the instigator of the assassination may have been Stalin himself. There were those in the Party who favoured Kirov as a possible alternative to Stalin as General Secretary, though it is highly unlikely that Kirov was himself involved in any specific challenge or plot. Whatever the exact circumstances – and they may never be known – Stalin used Kirov's murder as the pretext for the immediate introduction of a series of extraordinary anti-terrorist measures and an extensive purge of those suspected of complicity in the affair. The most prominent of the arrested suspects were former Politburo members, Kamenev and Zinoviev. In January 1935 they were tried and sentenced to imprisonment for allegedly maintaining a terrorist 'Centre' in Moscow and exercising ideological influence over Kirov's assassin. Other, less prominent suspects were summarily executed by the secret police, the NKVD (People's Commissariat for Internal Affairs). This was the beginning of the sinister process of political and physical blood-letting over the next four years, which is often referred to as 'The Great Terror'.

The public manifestation of this Soviet holocaust were the notorious show trials staged in Moscow between 1936 and 1938. At the first, in August 1936, Zinoviev, Kamenev and others were hauled from their cells in the Lubyanka (NKVD headquarters) to confess to a catalogue of crimes against the people, including plotting with the exiled Trotsky to murder Stalin and other members of the Politburo. There was no material evidence brought against them and no defence. The accused confessed their guilt and were immediately shot. During their confessions from the dock they had implicated others in their crimes, including Bukharin and members of the former Right Opposition. Their arrest and trial was only a matter of time.

At the second major trial, in 1937, other once-respected old Bolsheviks confessed to similar charges and met a similar fate. Finally, in March 1938, 'the trial of the 21' took place at which Bukharin, Rykov and former NKVD chief Genrikh Yagoda (1891–1938) – who had earlier set up the trial of Zinoviev and Kamenev! – faced the state prosecutor, the odious ex-Menshevik Andrei Vyshinsky (1885–1954). In addition to the 'normal' charges of maintaining links with Trotsky, plotting murder and industrial sabotage, Bukharin and company were accused of conspiring with foreign intelligence agencies to sell out parts of the Soviet Union to imperialist Japan and Nazi Germany. Bukharin actually dared to deny some of the charges in detail, but his general confession was sufficient to earn him the NKVD's by now routine bullet in the back of the skull. In the words of the official history of the Communist Party, published in 1939:

> These contemptible lackeys of the fascists forgot that the Soviet people had only to move a finger, and not a trace of them would be left.
> The Soviet court sentenced the Bukharin–Trotsky fiends to be shot.
> The People's Commissariat of Internal Affairs carried out the sentence.
> The Soviet people approved the annihilation of the Bukharin–Trotsky gang and moved on to next business.

It is worth considering briefly why these old comrades of Lenin should have confessed to such patently absurd charges. Apart from the application of torture, threats to wives and family, and the use of sophisticated, disorienting interrogation techniques, one should also bear in mind that all the accused were both ideologically and psychologically devoted to the Party. Deeply ingrained in them was the utter conviction that the Party could not ultimately be wrong. Some indeed may also have come actually to believe in their own guilt, and that in some way what was happening to them was for the good of socialism. This phenomenon of 'party-mindedness' (*partiinost*) is brilliantly portrayed in the figure of Rubashov, the central character in Arthur Koestler's chilling novel, *Darkness at Noon*, whose personality and political mentality are said to be modelled on Nikolai Bukharin. The Moscow trials were only the tip of a gigantic iceberg, the dimensions of which can only be guessed at. Only those whom the security forces, the NKVD interrogators, and the public prosecutor knew would confess in open court, would play their part, and repeat their lines in this macabre masquerade of justice actually made it to the dock. Otherwise the show would flop.

Behind the scenes, however, the agents of the NKVD conducted a huge drag-net operation, scouring the country for all known and suspected associates, colleagues, relatives and acquaintances of the central characters. In the interrogation chambers of the Lubyanka prison in Moscow and in police cells throughout Russia, tens, hundreds of thousands of bewildered, frightened citizens, loyal communists, dedicated revolutionaries and party functionaries found themselves victims of the dreaded pre-dawn knock and their anonymous accusers. The memoirs of those who survived make harrowing reading. Sophisticated interrogation techniques, physical and mental torture, deprivation of sleep, threats to close relatives and the administration of narcotic drugs were used with deadly finesse to weed out and destroy the 'enemies of the people'. The concepts of guilt by association, guilt by category, guilt by occupation, guilt by admission and guilt by silence were introduced as a means of widening the murderous trawl. Many foreign comrades, having fled to the bastion of socialism from their persecutors in fascist Europe, now suspect *because* they were foreign, sat and pondered the cruel irony of their fate in Stalin's dungeons.

The shock-waves soon reverberated far beyond the party *apparat*. Government officials, members of the diplomatic corps, leaders of national minorities, teachers of foreign languages, journalists and leading academics suffered in the onslaught on the intelligentsia. In 1938 the Red Army was literally decapitated by a military purge which swept away almost all its senior staff and commanding officers on the eve of a major war (much, incidentally, to Hitler's satisfaction). This was Stalin's inimitable way of preparing the Red Army for the possibility of war – purging it of its finest and most experienced military officers to make it an ideologically more trustworthy body. Not even the internal security services themselves were immune. Yagoda, author of the first purge trial, was arrested and replaced as head of the NKVD by Nikolai Yezhov (1895–1939?), 'the blood-thirsty dwarf', whose name has become synonymous with the terror, still known in Russia as the *Yezhovshchina*. Ultimately, Yezhov himself was sacked and his place taken by the no less repulsive Lavrenty Beria (1899–1953), Stalin's fellow Georgian, who was given the task of 'purging the purgers', a job he undertook with lethal relish. Yezhov himself disappeared, probably shot.

It is now traditional to note at this stage that the final victim of the Great Terror was Lev Trotsky, murdered in 1940 in far-off Mexico when one of Stalin's agents buried an ice-pick in his brain.

The terror of the 1930s was, of course, a nightmare phenomenon which nevertheless actually happened. And, like all nightmares, its reasons and its meaning are difficult to unravel or interpret. For millions it meant, of course, imprisonment, torture, execution, or the living death of exile in the charnel-house of Stalin's concentration camps, damningly immortalized in Alexander Solzhenitsyn's work as *The Gulag Archipelago* (GULag is the Russian abbreviation for the Main Prison Camp Administration, a department of the NKVD's empire). The stark horror of the camps is captured in their description by one of the survivors as 'Auschwitz without the ovens'. The ranks of the victims are legion.

For the Communist Party, the terror meant an almost complete change of personnel, the physical annihilation of the 'Old Bolsheviks' and their replacement by a whole new generation of reliable, unques-tioning and unimaginative sycophants who owed their lives and their careers to their willingness to step into dead men's shoes. These were a different breed of Communists from the heroes of the Revolution, creatures of Stalin who had been unnaturally selected through a process of the survival of the dullest.

For the peasantry, the terror – of which the horrors of collect-ivization were an integral part – literally revolutionized their lives far more radically than the events of 1917. Having lived and laboured for generations in communally organized extended family units (the *dvor*, 'household'), those who were not forcibly transported elsewhere were driven into what were essentially state-run, rather than collectively operated, *latifundia* subject to political control and the orders of pro-fessional agronomists. This new regimen led to the atrophy of the peasants' traditional *modus operandi* mentioned above. It must be remembered that peasants still constituted the large majority of the population, which meant that the majority of the population had what may be called a peasant mentality. This was one which still retained a traditional respect for authority (whether the *barin* [master], *pop* [priest], tsar or, indeed, God); a world-view which was at most provincial and at the least parochial; a 'culture' of land-cultivation and Christianity, tinctured with a residual belief in witchcraft and magic. Moshe Lewin has argued that, when several millions of peasants poured into the towns and cities during the industrialization drive, they brought with them their rural attitudes and superstitions, and were therefore responsible for a 'ruralization' of the urban centres and the new occupations and professions for which they were rapidly, though imperfectly, trained. The 'city-peasants' also responded to the pseudo-religious practices, festivals and rituals of the new state ideology and the 'leader-cult', which only facilitated the reinforcement of neo-autocratic control of society.

It also meant the emasculation of the intelligentsia and the rape of Soviet science and culture. Poets and playwrights, novelists and newspapermen, musicians and mathematicians, scientists and sculptors were selectively torn from their professional environments and subjected to systematic persecution, humiliation or exile. Those who refused to conform to the rigid cultural commandments of the regime became martyrs to a mediocracy of philistinism and intellectual sterility in which they were either muzzled or murdered. Even technical experts were executed when natural disasters or failures occurred – for example, veterinary specialists blamed for cattle disease, or meteorologists for drought. That is not to say that absolutely nothing of creative or scientific merit emerged during this period, but what did survive were oases in an artistic desert.

For many national minorities it meant mass deportation from their traditional homelands and the decapitation of the national elites. Although this policy of what nowadays is sometimes referred to as 'ethnic cleansing' did not occur on a massive scale until Hitler's invasion of the USSR in 1941, sweeping measures had already been inaugurated in the early and mid-1930s that marked a significant break from the more practical and enlightened approach to the nationalities problem pursued during the 1920s. The collectivization campaign involved the concentration on single-crop cultivation and the establishment of huge cotton plantations in Central Asia, the sedentarization of nomadic herders, and the compulsory education (in Russian) of their children in boarding schools (Russian, *internat*), which isolated the growing generation not only from the language, but also from the traditional skills, occupations and crafts of their native peoples. At the height of the purges (1936–38), almost the entire national leadership of the Communist Party in the non-Russian republics was exterminated and replaced by ethnic Russians. For example, the *whole* of the Ukrainian Politburo was eliminated, and only a handful of the Central Committee survived. Members of the national intelligentsias were viewed by the central authorities with particular suspicion as the articulators of national particularism, and similarly purged out of existence. Manifestations of old loyalties, former allegiances, national identities and cultural and political affiliations were suppressed as Stalin sought to bring everyone 'into line' as part of his policy of centralization of power, elimination of separate initiative, coordination and homogenization. In many ways, it was reminiscent of Hitler's campaign of *Gleichschaltung*, which imposed allegiance to national socialism, the Third Reich and the Führer. The adoption of a new national anthem (the 'State Hymn of the Soviet Union'), with its emphasis on 'Great Russia' (*Velikaya Rus'*) creating an indestructible union of 'free' republics, also re-emphasized the relationship between the national minorities and 'Mother [or "Big Brother"(?)] Russia'. As mentioned above, the process climaxed during the Second World War with the wholesale transportation in cattle-wagons of entire nationalities – Kalmyks, the Caucasian Balkars, Ingush, Chechens, Crimean Tatars, Meshketians, as well as Koreans and Volga Germans – into Siberia or Central Asia as potential collaborators with the invading enemy. Only long after Stalin's death were these peoples allowed to return to their original homelands. The non-Russians' legacy of long pent-up resentment and hostility to the imperial policies of both tsars and Soviets was a vitally – or lethally? – fissiparous force in the eventual collapse of the Soviet Union.

For Stalin himself, his Great Terror meant the elimination of his rivals and critics – past, present and potential, real or imagined, the ultimate consolidation of his tyrannical power and the establishment of the cult of his own personality (see Chapter 7). And, finally, for the Soviet people it meant decades of fear, suspicion, ignorance of their own past and the outside world, and an almost fatalistic submissiveness to the totalitarian system which he created, but to which they succumbed.

Interpretations

To seek rational explanations for such an irrational and complex phenomenon as the Great Terror is a superhuman task. Some writers regard Stalin's blood purge as the logical and unavoidable consequence of original Bolshevik theory and practice. In this view, Lenin's advocacy of an élite, highly centralized and disciplined hierarchical party must inevitably give rise to the tyranny of a single dictator, as Trotsky had predicted as early as 1904 (see Chapter 3). Lenin was not by nature squeamish in his methods of dealing with opposition, and personally signed thousands of death warrants consigning his enemies to their fate, including the last tsar and his family. In December 1917, he established the Extraordinary Commission for the Struggle against Counter-revolution and Sabotage (the *Cheka*), scourge of anti-Bolsheviks and the class enemy, and in 1921 introduced his 'Resolution on Party Unity', proscribing organized opposition factions within the Party. Both of these tools, in the shape of the NKVD and the excommunication of his political rivals, were to be used by Stalin with ultimately deadly effect. However, there is nothing in the body of Lenin's writings or political philosophy that authorizes, condones or envisages the systematic suppression or slaughter of several millions of totally guiltless, indeed loyal, citizens.

Others have suggested that the premature nature of the Russian Revolution, which sought to create a highly industrialized socialist society in a backward, peasant country, necessitated the use of coercion to achieve the revolution's objectives. Whether apocryphal or not, Stalin is reputed once to have commented that 'one cannot make an omelette without breaking eggs'. Implicitly, one cannot build socialism without breaking lots of heads. But again, there is a qualitative difference between the use of violence in a revolutionary situation and the cold-blooded, deliberate extermination of whole sections of the population in peacetime. As indicated in Chapter 3, millions perished in the carnage of the Civil War, but, tragically, that is precisely in the nature of war, whether international or civil. Even more tragically, not only military casualties, but also the killing of civilians and non-combatants is an inevitable consequence of armed mass conflict – what is sometimes euphemistically termed 'collateral damage'. But what happened during Stalin's terror was of a radically different nature. The country was *not* at war, though the collectivization had taken on the proportions of an all-out civil war against the peasants. Nevertheless, at the height of the purges millions of Soviet citizens were condemned simply by category, status or occupation, as were their associates, neighbours or friends, all branded as 'enemies of the people', denounced, disgraced and dispatched to their doom.

The exact numbers of the terror's victims can of course never be known, and the topic has been the subject of much historiographical and demographic debate. As the Cambridge historian, Chris Ward, has pointed out, the first problem in calculating the figures is one of definition and chronology. Should the historian confine himself/ herself to the 'high terror' between 1936 and 1939 – that is, between the first major show trial and the 18th Party Congress when Stalin, declaring the mass purges over, described them as 'unavoidable, but beneficial'? Or, should one start with Kirov's murder in 1934, or even with the as yet bloodless purges of 1932 (e.g. the expulsion of supporters of Mikhail Riutin, organizer of an anti-Stalin caucus within the Party, and the trial of alleged industrial saboteurs)? Does one include all those who starved to death during collectivization and those who were worked to death in the camps? What about those who endured unspeakable torments, but then survived? In other words, should the victims who were arrested, exiled, imprisoned, executed or otherwise 'repressed' all count for equal value in this macabre mathematical equation? The consensus of recent scholarly opinion, supported by the evidence of KGB archives released during the period of *glasnost*, inclines to the view that the total was not as high as some of the more alarmist earlier accounts had suggested. For instance, Robert Conquest's estimate of over twenty million victims has been persuasively challenged on purely demographic grounds. The whole problem is of course befuddled by dodgy statistics, political prejudice and ephemeral ideological fads, imperfect memories and mistaken assumptions. Even prominent and highly respected western scholars have admitted to having made numerical miscalculations. But in the final analysis, do the precise figures really matter? The sheer scale of the terror, on whatever accounting system, whether the numbers are in the millions or tens of millions, is nevertheless sickeningly grotesque and must surely count as one of the most evil manifestations of man's inhumanity to man in history.

But be that as it may, Stalin did not perpetrate his crimes alone and unaided. He had – to borrow a term from the history of Hitler's Germany – his 'willing executioners' – that is, hundreds of thousands of agents and operatives, not just in the higher echelons of the NKVD, but throughout the entire Soviet system. Apart from active and direct participants – prison guards, lawyers, drivers, clerks, railway workers, local officials, doctors, and other essential cogs in the machinery of suppression – there were also millions of ordinary Soviet citizens who were either to turn a blind eye, acquiesce or even take advantage of the operation. Again, to make an analogy with the historiography of Nazi Germany, it is possible to replicate the so-called 'intentionalist versus structuralist' debate concerning Hitler's personal role in the holocaust, and apply it to Stalin's Russia. In this case, the intentionalists' view is that from the outset Stalin deliberately planned the Great Terror as a means of imposing his will on Soviet society by means of massive coercion and the institutionalization of fear, as described and discussed above. Whether or not the goal of creating a 'totally totalitarian' system was achieved is in a sense neither here nor there, but *that*, say the intentionalists, was the intention. This view of Stalin's crimes is now shared by many post-Soviet Russian historians and intellectuals who find it convenient to attribute the horrors of the past to the machiavellian stratagems of a malign dictator and his evil minions. In this way, the victimized Russian masses are absolved from any blame for participating in the ghastly operation.

More recently, a new school of western, mainly American, scholars has evolved a 'revisionist' methodology that approaches the terror by examining the interplay between state and society, by investigating the lives, responses and attitudes of 'ordinary' citizens, and by focusing its attention not on ideology, politics or personality, but on social groups and structures at grassroots and local level. These – investigators such as Fitzpatrick, Getty, Manning, Rittersporn, Thurston *et al.* (see 'Suggestions for further reading') – are the social historians of Stalinism, the 'structuralists'.

They argue that the terror did not occur in a vacuum, and that 'Stalinism flowered in a responsive soil'. The active nutrients in this soil were not just willing Communist *apparatchiki*, government officials and NKVD-ists, but middle managers, rank-and-file Party members, working-class enthusiasts, radical opponents of bureaucracy, Stakhanovites and millions of 'ordinary' people. Indeed, it was precisely the élite of the Soviet social, political and military system that bore the main brunt of the terror, and Robert Thurston in his book offers many examples of popular *Schadenfreude* at the spectacle of top Party members 'cutting each other's throats'. Many also no doubt seized the opportunity to exact vengeance on local officials who had abused their authority, or to settle old personal scores. There is here no attempt to minimize the sheer scope and horror of the purges, but what is suggested is that the large *majority* of the population was untouched by them, or else were willing to accept that there were in fact wreckers, saboteurs and traitors at large, internal enemies who needed to be rooted out, investigated and punished. The primary aim of the terror was not, according to this argument, to terrorize the whole of society – indeed, the task of monitoring the activities, movements and opinions of the entire population was clearly impossible – but to investigate perceived offences. Stalin, grotesquely paranoid as he was, genuinely believed in the existence of enemies and plotters, and sought to exterminate them. There was, however, no grand plan. Thurston concludes that the terror simply 'assumed a momentum and dynamic of its own among the populace. Neither Stalin nor the NKVD acted independently of society'. This interpretation is in many ways more disturbing than the traditional one. It suggests that large sections of Soviet society, while going about their own everyday business, consciously or unconsciously contributed to the construction of Stalinism. In this scenario, to be sure, Stalin appears as protagonist, but with a supporting cast of millions.

It is, too, interesting to note that even highly sophisticated people who knew something about what was going on were persuaded, or managed to persuade themselves, that somehow Stalin himself was not personally to blame for what was happening; that it was all the doing of Yezhov and the NKVD. The writer, Ilya Ehrenburg, tells in his memoirs of an occasion at the height of the *Yezhovshchina* when he met the poet Boris Pasternak one snowy night in Moscow. He related how Pasternak raised his arms to the skies and cried, 'If only someone would tell Stalin about all this!' There were many others also believed that Stalin was being kept in the dark. This is reminiscent of the naïve faith that the common people of pre-Revolutionary Russia had in a benevolent tsar who was kept in ignorance of their suffering by scheming bureaucrats and rapacious landlords.

There is also the foreign dimension to be taken into consideration, and many scholars have pointed to the exigencies of the international situation during the 1930s. To preserve the territorial and political integrity of the USSR against the threat of European fascism and Nazism, it was essential to ensure that internally the country remained strongly united and that all potential sources of political opposition that might have weakened the Soviet system from within be eliminated at all costs. The victory of the Red Army over the Germans at the battle of Stalingrad in 1943 – so runs this argument – proved that Stalin's policies were right. On the other hand, it has been fairly objected that, 'but for Stalin's policies, the Germans would not have got as far as Stalingrad'! Indeed, one might go further to suggest that, but for Stalin's policies, the Germans might never have dared to cross the Soviet frontier in the first place.

Finally there is the psychological interpretation that attributes Stalin's terror simply to the paranoid machinations of a criminally deranged psychopath, of a morbidly suspicious and vindictive megalomaniac suffering from the combination of an inferiority complex and delusions of grandeur mixed with homicidal tendencies. Clearly, his behaviour was far from normal, but the present author – like many of those who *have* confidently offered such a diagnosis – is not medically qualified to give an authoritative opinion on the clinical aspects of the case. (Those interested in the more intimate details of Stalin's private life and mental state are referred to Simon Montefiore's recent book, *Stalin: The Court of the Red Tsar* – see 'Suggestions for further reading'.) Recently, a hypothesis has been put forward which suggests that the purges should be seen as a natural disaster like a flood or tempest that periodically sweeps through a land, ravaging the population and destroying everything in its path. Unlike the forces of nature, however, the causes of human tragedies must be sought in the activities of human beings. Unfortunately, none of the explanations of the Great Terror so far advanced by historians, political scientists or psychoanalysts may be regarded as wholly safe or satisfactory.

In 1939 the purges were declared to be over. In the same year Stalin's Commissar for Foreign Affairs, Vyacheslav Molotov (1890–1986), signed a treaty of mutual non-aggression with his German opposite number, von Ribbentrop. While Europe was at war, the infamous *Pakt* was to buy the Soviet Union two years of relative peace before she was hurled into yet another nightmare of horror and unimaginable suffering in the shape of the Nazi invasion under the code-name 'Barbarossa'.

5

The military leader

Barbarossa

Very little has so far been said about Stalin's conduct of foreign policy. During the 1920s the Soviet Union pursued an ambiguous and seemingly contradictory course in its relations with the outside world. On the one hand, she needed to establish a peaceful working relationship with the hostile capitalist powers with which she was surrounded, if possible gaining diplomatic recognition and establishing overseas trade links. On the other hand, the government was still ideologically committed to the concept of world revolution and the overthrow of the capitalist system with which it was, nevertheless, striving peacefully to co-exist. To this end, Lenin had inaugurated the Third (Communist) International (*Comintern*) in March 1919. However, it soon became apparent that, as in its dealings with foreign governments, so with foreign communist parties, the immediate national self-interest of the Soviet Union was paramount and took precedence over the long-term ideological goal of international communism. Lenin's disputes with the so-called Left Communists over the treaty of Brest-Litovsk established the precedent (see Chapter 3), and Stalin was later to reinforce the primacy of nationalist over internationalist aims with his policy of Socialism in One Country, even if this meant abandoning foreign comrades in favour of alliances with moderate political parties. In China, this policy ended in tragedy in 1927 when the Comintern-backed nationalist forces of Chiang Kai-shek's Kuomintang butchered the Chinese communists in Shanghai.

In Europe, Stalin's policy towards the German Communist Party can be seen in retrospect to have been equally tragic, though for different reasons and with more calamitous repercussions for the security of the Soviet Union. In close step with his 1928 left wheel in domestic policies, through the Comintern Stalin ordered that there should be no political or electoral alliance between communist and other left-wing or socialist parties. The German Social Democrats were smeared with political abuse as 'social fascists' even when the example of Mussolini's Italy had already given warning of the danger from the extreme right, and when the German National Socialist (*Nazi*) Party was gaining strength in the dying days of the Weimar Republic. While not itself directly responsible, this ultra-sectarian policy towards the left certainly facilitated the electoral victory of Adolf Hitler (1889–1945) as German Chancellor in 1933. But still Stalin underestimated the menace of fascism and Nazism, and continued with his myopic vilification of Europe's non-communist left.

In 1935 the seventh congress of the Third International convened in Moscow, at which Stalin unashamedly announced a U-turn in Comintern policy. Hitler's aggressive domestic and foreign policies had finally persuaded Stalin where the real danger lay and prompted him to order the formation of 'popular fronts' of all parties of the left, centre and even moderate right to combat the evils of fascism and National Socialism in Europe. In his speeches Hitler had made no secret of his racialist contempt for the 'subhuman' Slavs as well as his political hatred of bolshevism; nor did he conceal his territorial ambitions in the East, where Soviet Ukraine would provide ample 'living space' (*Lebensraum*) for the master race of conquering Aryans. Against this threat, Stalin sought the collective security of an alliance with the European democracies to pave the way for joint action, especially with Britain and France, to contain Germany. They, however, seemed more intent on appeasing Hitler's militant ambitions and standing meekly by – or, indeed, actively collaborating – as the Führer steadily expanded the power of the Third Reich across the continent.

The remilitarization of the Rhineland, the anti-Comintern pact of Germany, Italy and Japan, the annexation of Austria, and German–Italian aid to Franco's rebel forces during the Spanish Civil War were sufficient examples of Hitler's aggressive intentions and his determination to put them into effect. Simultaneous confrontation with imperial Japan in the Far East faced the Soviet Union with the possibility of having to fight a war on two fronts, and Stalin with the problem of how to avoid it. In 1938 Russia was deliberately excluded from the negotiations in Munich which led to Hitler's dismemberment of Czechoslovakia. Stalin now had to think fast and hard. The western powers had more or less abandoned republican Spain to its fate. Independent Czechoslovakia had been sacrificed on the altar of appeasement. The Red Army high command had been all but obliterated in Stalin's purge. Soviet troops were already fighting the Japanese at the battles of Lake Khasan and Khalkhin-Gol in the Far East. What guarantee was there that a formal military alliance against Hitler would bring Britain and France speeding to Moscow's aid in case of a German attack? Unfortunately, there were many circles in Europe who thought that this would be no bad thing. Procrastination and lack of purpose marked the French and British responses to Russia's offer of a Franco-British-Soviet anti-Nazi alliance. Finally, Stalin did the unthinkable. He concluded a pact with Hitler.

Looked at in terms of *Realpolitik* and the Soviet Union's own security, the Nazi–Soviet treaty of non-aggression was a sensible move. Morally and politically it outraged the European left and tore the 'popular front' to shreds. Militarily, it gave Hitler a free hand to launch the invasion of Poland. Britain and France declared war on Germany but initially took no direct action to rescue Poland. However, the Second World War had now begun.*

The *Pakt* did not turn the Soviet Union and Nazi Germany into allies. It simply guaranteed their mutual non-aggression. It also incidentally allowed Stalin to occupy parts of eastern Poland and reincorporate the Baltic republics of Estonia, Latvia and Lithuania into the Soviet Union. This was carried out with great brutality during 1939–40 and involved the enforced 'sovietization' of all public and private institutions and the mass deportation of thousands of Balts and Poles to Siberia and Central Asia. (Over 14,000 Polish army officers were massacred and buried in mass graves at Katyn in Belorussia, an atrocity that was almost certainly carried out by Soviet security forces and for which Gorbachev later apologized.) The ostensible reason for all this activity was the strengthening of the Soviet Union's western defences, a policy that was further pursued during the 'Winter War' of 1939–40 against Finland. The courageous Finns put up a bitter and sustained resistance but were eventually forced to cede considerable territory to the Soviet invaders.

---

* Ruth Henig, *The Origins of the Second World War 1933–1939*, Lancaster Pamphlets, Routledge, London, 2nd edn, 1994.

For almost two years after the *Pakt* was signed, anti-Nazi propaganda was played down in the Soviet Union, Russo-German commercial and diplomatic relations continued, and the country was lulled into a false sense of security. However, having made himself master of continental Europe, Hitler once more turned his thoughts towards the East. It is clear that plans to attack the Soviet Union were being laid soon after the fall of France in June 1940, but Stalin unaccountably refused to heed the warnings of reliable intelligence sources concerning Hitler's intentions. German troop and naval deployments, information from espionage circles in occupied Europe, from defecting German soldiers, from Winston Churchill, and from the Soviet master-spy Richard Sorge in Tokyo – Stalin chose to ignore them all, and dismissed as 'provocative' the advice of his senior military officers to mobilize.

At 0415 on Sunday 22 June 1941 Hitler struck. The German armies invaded on a broad front with a three-pronged lightning assault (*Blitzkrieg*) aimed at Leningrad in the north, Moscow in the centre, and Kiev and Ukraine to the south. As their tanks raced virtually unopposed across Soviet territory, *Luftwaffe* bombs demolished the Soviet airforce before its planes could even leave the ground. The onslaught took the Russian people completely by surprise. Army command was paralysed through lack of orders. Stalin was stunned. Operation Barbarossa – 'the biggest military operation ever mounted' – was under way.

Stalingrad

This is not the place to give a blow-by-blow account of the Nazi–Soviet conflict. Some details are, however, necessary. By the early autumn the country was in a totally demoralized state. The *Wehrmacht* had penetrated swiftly and deeply into Soviet territory. The whole of Belorussia and parts of Ukraine were in enemy hands. Millions of prisoners were taken. Leningrad was besieged and in the grip of a murderous blockade during which over a million of its citizens were to perish in horrifying conditions – more than the total combined British and American casualties in the entire war. One after another, major Soviet cities fell – Minsk, Smolensk, Riga, Tallin, Pskov, Kiev, Kharkov, Odessa – until by mid-October German troops were in the outskirts of Moscow, only a few kilometres from the Kremlin.

The astonishing speed of the German advance was facilitated by a number of factors: the surprise of the attack and the unpreparedness of the Soviet forces; Stalin's obstinacy in refusing to believe it was imminent; the superior equipment and armour of the German troops; the low morale of the population, which had barely recovered from the rigours of collectivization, the five-year plans and the purge (in some areas the Germans were initially greeted as liberators); and, finally, the poor quality and inexperience of the officer corps – a direct result of the recent purge of the military high command. Nor did the 'scorched earth' policy carried out by the retreating Russian soldiers create a major obstacle. On 3 July Stalin addressed the nation with a speech in which he called for the destruction of everything that might be of use to the invader:

> the enemy must not be left a single engine, a single railway truck, not a single pound of grain or gallon of fuel . . . In occupied areas, partisan units must be formed, sabotage groups must be formed . . . to blow up bridges and roads, damage telephone and telegraph wires, set fire to forests, stores and transport . . . conditions must be made intolerable for the enemy and all his accomplices.

Where there was time, factories, plant, machinery and their work-forces were uprooted and shipped eastwards to be relocated in the vast hinterland beyond the Urals. As if in replication of Lenin's policy at Brest-Litovsk, Stalin was in effect sacrificing space to buy time: time to recover from the shock of invasion, to regather the country's strength, to work out strategy, to gear the whole nation – man, woman and child – to the war effort, and time to carry out delicate diplomatic manoeuvres with the Soviet Union's new, unlikely, allies, first Britain and then the United States.

The battle for Moscow was launched in October and raged throughout November and the first days of December. The German forces were over-extended and ill-equipped to deal with the rigours of a particularly atrocious Russian winter. Warm clothing was in short supply; fuel froze in its tanks; leather German jackboots cracked apart and thousands died of frostbite as General (later Marshal) Zhukov, commander of the western front, launched a savage counter-offensive, reinforced by snow-toughened Siberian troops fresh from the Far Eastern front. Moscow was saved. The Germans fell back 150 kilometres and Stalin reaped the glory.

The defence of Moscow, which Stalin never left, was a tremendous morale-booster for the Soviet people as a whole and for Stalin in particular. The entire country was united as it had not been united since before the Revolution. A superhuman effort was made to increase armaments production and reconstitute industrial war losses. Old enemies were rehabilitated and released from the camps. Even the Russian Orthodox Church was later restored to favour as a reward for its patriotic efforts and appeals for the defence of 'Holy Russia'. The victories of past heroes like Prince Alexander Nevsky, Dmitry Donskoy, Minin and Pozharsky, and General Kutuzov were celebrated in official propaganda and constant analogies drawn between Hitler's invasion and Napoleon's ill-fated campaign of 1812. Tolstoy's great novel *War and Peace* was reprinted in thousands of cheap editions to remind people of their former triumph. Tchaikovsky's *1812 Overture* constantly blasted out from public loudspeakers. The whole of Russian society, soldier and factoryhand, peasant and party official, stood shoulder-to-shoulder to defend Russia in what is still referred to as the 'Great Patriotic War'.

Paradoxically, perhaps, wartime saw a number of further relaxations in official policy. Restrictions on party membership were loosened as millions of new members hurried to join its ranks; literature briefly flourished as authors filled their books with epics of patriotic endeavour; the Comintern was disbanded in deference to the new alliance with the western democracies; and in its propaganda the government toned down the ideological antagonism between socialism and capitalism, calling on the allies to defend democracy against fascism. Not that propaganda was necessary to stir up patriotic enthusiasm; the barbaric, racially inspired treatment of the civilian population by the invaders was more than sufficient to inflame anti-German hatred to fever pitch. Villages were razed to the ground, women and children raped and tortured, Jews, communists and ordinary Russians systematically butchered as Hitler's agents carried out his genocidal policies which officially cast the Slavs as 'subhuman' (*Untermenschen*), fit only for slavery or slaughter.

To their cost, the German armies were soon to discover the almost superhuman, fanatical fighting qualities of the Russian soldier in the battle which was to become the decisive turning-point in the war. Having failed to take Moscow, and with Leningrad still suffering the horrors of the continuing siege, Hitler concentrated his attentions on the southern front. The whole of Ukraine was overrun and for a moment it looked as if the Caucasus would suffer a similar fate. However, Hitler made the fatal decision to throw his armies at the city on the River Volga which bore Stalin's name – Stalingrad.

Tactically speaking, Stalingrad (the old Tsaritsyn, scene of Stalin's civil war contretemps) was not a vital objective, but Hitler seemed to be mesmerized by the prospect of destroying 'Stalin's city'. By August 1942 his troops were in the suburbs, encircling the town and squeezing the Soviet 62nd Army with its back to the river. Throughout the autumn and winter of 1942–43 the greatest and fiercest battle of the Second World War was fought in the streets and houses of a single town. For Stalin and for the entire nation Stalingrad epitomized the burden of the war which the Soviet Union felt it was bearing single-handed. Certainly the western allies' failure to open up the promised second front in Europe in 1942 meant that Hitler could concentrate his attention on the east, forcing Russia to bear the brunt of the hostilities for another two years.

It is impossible to convey the horror and the heroism, the courage and the carnage of Stalingrad in so little space. Street-to-street, room-to-room and hand-to-hand combat raged with a savage intensity in which, to quote Isaac Deutscher, 'the conquest of a single street cost the Germans as much time and blood as they had hitherto spent on the conquest of entire European countries'. Hitler fulminated that there should be no retreat. Stalin issued his famous command, 'Not one step back!' Gradually the dogged Russian resistance turned into a fierce counter-offensive. General von Paulus's 6th Army was surrounded by a Soviet pincer movement and cut off from its Italian and Romanian reinforcements to the west. Hitler insisted frantically on no surrender, but finally the exhausted, decimated Germans were forced into submission. Von Paulus capitulated on 2 February 1943. With him twenty-four generals and nearly 100,000 men were captured, leaving another 70,000 German dead in the ruins of Stalingrad. An almost equal number of Russians lay with them.

Stalin was triumphant. In March he assumed the rank of Marshal of the Soviet Union and later Winston Churchill presented him with a ceremonial sword from the British monarch, King George VI, as a mark of his personal esteem for the Soviet feat of arms. The victory on the Volga had shown that the *Wehrmacht* was no longer invincible. The tide of war had changed.

Victory

The battle was won, but another two years of devastating warfare were to follow before the occupied areas were liberated and Nazi Germany defeated. Stalingrad was a crushing personal blow for Hitler. His mental and psychological deterioration after the defeat seemed to be matched by the slow, inexorable collapse of his eastern front as the Red Army drove relentlessly westwards. But the German army was still a formidable opponent and many major battles remained to be fought, including the battle for Kursk in July 1943, which turned out to be the biggest tank battle of the Second World War. The roll-call of cities that had fallen to the Germans in 1941–42 was now put into reverse as Ukraine and Belorussia were gradually liberated during 1943 and 1944. In the north the murderous siege of Leningrad was finally lifted early in 1944, and by the summer Soviet troops were pushing into Poland and the Balkans with the Germans in full retreat well before the allied landings in Normandy finally opened the second front. In May 1945 Red Army troops under the command of Marshals Koniev and Zhukov entered the German capital and planted the red flag on top of the Berlin Reichstag. The formal German surrender to the victorious allies was signed at Soviet army headquarters in Berlin on 8 May 1945 (9 May, Moscow time). The war in Europe was over.

Stalin was at the height of his power and popularity both at home and abroad. In June 1945 he adopted the title of 'Generalissimo' and was universally acknowledged as one of the great wartime leaders. In the closing stages of the war he had met on equal terms with the British Prime Minister, Churchill, and the American President, Roosevelt, at the allied conferences in Teheran (1943), Yalta and Potsdam (1945) at which the political boundaries of post-war Europe were drawn. During the negotiations, which Churchill was later to describe as a process of 'horse-trading', continental Europe was divided into respective 'zones' or 'spheres of influence' between the Soviet Union and the western powers. Germany itself, including Berlin, was carved up into British, American, French and Soviet sectors, while the over-whelming Red Army presence in eastern and south-eastern Europe guaranteed that these countries would remain firmly under Stalin's sway. Before the war the Soviet Union had been politically isolated, surrounded by the hostile 'capitalist encirclement' and intent on building Socialism in One Country. Stalin now bestrode half of a prostrate Europe and the Soviet Union was poised to emerge as one of the world's two military and political 'superpowers', which were soon to confront each other during the tense years of the 'Cold War'.

However, the flush of victory and the territorial and diplomatic gains in Eastern Europe could do little to solace the country's battered population, or what was left of it. From Russia's point of view, the war was probably the greatest pyrrhic victory in history. Initial estimates, only later released, indicated that 20 million of the Soviet population – more than one in ten – were killed, around half of them civilians and the majority of them males of the virile age-group. Recently released archival sources in the former USSR suggest that the total casualties may in fact have been far higher – as many as 27 or even 30 million. The resulting sexual imbalance and demographic consequences were to last for many years. Of those that survived, hundreds of thousands were left crippled, maimed and unfit for work. Apart from the physical mutilations, whole cohorts of Soviet citizens were left psychologically scarred for life. Indeed, the shocking slaughter left a deep and ineradicable trauma in the mind and soul of the Soviet people which has only quite recently begun to heal, though the visible and invisible scars still remain. The sheer scale of the human suffering and material destruction is unimaginable. Complete cities, towns, villages and settlements were obliterated, leaving around twenty-five million homeless. In Stalingrad, 90 per cent of the city was flattened. In Leningrad, more people died through shelling, cold or starvation than were killed by the American atomic bombs dropped on Hiroshima and Nagasaki. To anyone visiting the Piskarevskoye memorial cemetery in St Petersburg today the agony and the grief are almost tangible, as if congealed in the very atmosphere.

The victory was therefore bought at a terrible price, not only for the fighting men but also for the civilian population. Peace, however, brought only the briefest respite. As Stalin consolidated his grip on the countries of Eastern Europe and as the uneasy warmth of the Grand Alliance began to freeze and harden into the enmity of the Cold War, the long-suffering Soviet people now faced the Herculean task of national reconstruction, but in the face of renewed international hostility.

6

The Cold Warrior

Reconstruction

A physically decimated, debilitated and emotionally distraught nation was now called upon to restore its shattered economy. Over one-quarter of the industrial capacity of the Soviet Union had been destroyed, and in those areas occupied by the enemy the proportion was even higher, around 65 per cent. In particular, the heavy industries such as iron, steel and fuel, which had been given special emphasis during the five-year plans, were badly hit. Hundreds of factories, foundries, mines and workshops had been either devastated in the fighting or demolished by the scorched-earth policies of the retreating armies, both Russian and German. What could be saved had been transported east and relocated in a desperate programme of territorial diversification of industry which successfully enhanced production levels after the initial onslaught. Over 300 entire enterprises and their workforces were uprooted, trans-shipped and reassembled in Siberia.

Light industry had also suffered. During the war years all industry was geared to military or paramilitary output, with little or no spare capacity for consumer-goods production. This had, of course, been a feature of the pre-war economic priorities and the same pattern was now to be repeated in the new five-year plan for national reconstruction (1946–50), with a consequent continuation of material hardship, shortages of essential goods, and a depressed standard of living for the foreseeable future. The situation was exacerbated by the low priority given to the construction of domestic accommodation in favour of capital building and rebuilding projects and it was not until well into the 1950s that large-scale housing schemes got under way to alleviate the desperate shortage. Transport and communication networks had likewise been ruined and strenuous efforts had to be made to replace railways, rolling stock and blown-up bridges. Agriculture was in a shambles. In the occupied areas where farms had been decollectivized, a crash programme of recollectivization was instituted, but a combination of lack of manpower on the land, shortage of livestock and machinery, drought and dubious planning methods ensured that agriculture long remained the Achilles heel of the Soviet economy.

Despite the hardships and the sacrifices, progress was made. Some of the industrial losses were made good by the import of capital equipment from the defeated countries, in particular the Soviet sector of Germany, in the shape of reparations and war booty. Shortfalls in manpower were to some extent offset by utilizing the forced labour of prisoners of war, around two million of whom were detained in Soviet labour camps until long after the end of the war. Even Soviet prisoners of war returning home from captivity in Europe now found themselves once more behind barbed wire as Stalin punished them for having surrendered or succumbed to the enemy! The technological expertise of captured or commandeered foreign specialists and scientists was also made to contribute to the nation's recovery. They also assisted in the race to match the United States' recently demonstrated atomic weapons capability. But the major contribution to national revival was made by the spectacular exertions of the Soviet working population, which was called upon yet again to conquer almost insurmountable obstacles in what were still generally appalling conditions. Genuine enthusiasm to make good the war losses was reinforced by a return to the strict communal discipline and draconian methods of the 1930s. Stalin abandoned the relative relaxations of the war years and marshalled all the resources of the police state to reimpose the controls of his totalitarian system with a renewed vigour.

The cult of Stalin himself, already well established in the 1930s but now illuminated by the aureole of martial glory, assumed new dimensions. Extravagant, incredible, even ludicrous claims were made concerning his revolutionary zeal, his intellectual prowess, his economic achievements, his military leadership and his omniscient wisdom. Stalin was hailed as the Father of the Peoples, the Captain of Industry, the Closest Comrade-in-Arms of Lenin, the Great Educator, the Mighty Leader, even the Shining Sun! The panegyrics knew no bounds. This was not just hero-worship; this was Stalin's apotheosis.

No one dared query his word. Even his obsequious creatures on the party Politburo were, in Nikita Khrushchev's chilling phrase, only 'temporary people' who never knew on leaving Stalin's presence whether they would end up at home in bed or in the cells of the Lubyanka. At one of his increasingly frequent drinking bouts, Stalin once ordered the portly Khrushchev to dance the strenuously athletic Ukrainian *gopak*, squatting on his haunches and kicking out his heels. Khrushchev painfully but prudently obeyed. As he later observed to his fellow Politburo member Anastas Mikoyan, 'When Stalin says "Dance!", a wise man dances'.

Outside the closed circle of his political minions, the rest of the population also danced to Stalin's bidding. Apart from the toiling peasants and workers, members of the artistic and scientific intelligentsia were all compelled to perform according to the dictates of the master choreographer. One of the most serious casualties was the science of genetics, which was set back a whole generation because of Stalin's support for the ideologically convenient but scientifically spurious theories of the bogus biologist Trofim Lysenko, who claimed that acquired characteristics could be genetically transmitted. Only mathematics and physics seemed to be safe from interference, no doubt because of their strategic and military applications.

In the humanities, linguistics, philosophy and even music were forced into the Stalinist straitjacket, but it was literature that bore the brunt of Stalin's renewed attack on creative freedom. The 'Great Educator's' chief hatchet-man in the artistic abattoir of the late 1940s was Andrei Zhdanov (1896–1948), the man who had succeeded the murdered Kirov as boss of the Leningrad party organization in 1934. In 1946 the so-called 'Zhdanov decrees' were promulgated, which introduced a period of such cultural sterility and talentless uniformity as to outrival even the 'socialist realist' mediocrities of the 1930s. After closing down two Leningrad journals for publishing material that allegedly 'kowtowed' to western literary fashion, Zhdanov singled out two writers for especially vicious abuse and public humiliation, Mikhail Zoshchenko, a writer of satirical short stories, and the popular lyric poetess and veteran of the Leningrad siege, Anna Akhmatova. The intensely personal love themes and religious imagery of much of Akhmatova's verse led Zhdanov to pillory her as 'part nun, part whore', who divided her time between the convent and the brothel. The crude invective apart, the extreme nationalism with which

Zhdanov's campaign was suffused was not without its anti-Semitic overtones, and many Jewish intellectuals, condemned as Zionists or 'rootless cosmopolitans', disappeared in the arid cultural wilderness of the *Zhdanovshchina*. In a sense the intense philistinism, paranoia and xenophobia of this post-war period of 'high Stalinism' was an internal reflection of the rapidly deteriorating relations between the Soviet Union and the West in the early years of the Cold War.

Cold War

Rivers of ink have flowed in an attempt to trace and analyse the origins of the Cold War, which in many ways dominated the course of international relations throughout the world in the second half of the twentieth century. Many regional conflicts in far-flung areas of the globe are impossible to understand except in the context of the political, ideological and military confrontation between the Soviet Union and her allies on the one hand and the United States and the western powers on the other. How did the wartime allies become peacetime antagonists, threatening to bring the world to the brink of a nuclear Armageddon?

Many historians trace the origins of the Cold War right back to the Bolshevik Revolution of 1917, which the capitalist countries regarded as a direct threat to their own political stability and economic security. (Hence Churchill's call to throttle the infant monster, mentioned earlier.) In this interpretation, the wartime alliance was a temporary aberration forced on the participating countries by the shared menace of German Nazism, and the post-war slide into non-belligerent hostility merely a resumption of 'normal' relations. While there is much force in this argument, one must also seek the more immediate causes of the mutual suspicion, mistrust and outright animosity during the last few years of Stalin's life.

At the conferences of Teheran and Yalta, as already indicated, some kind of loose agreement was reached among the 'Big Three' on the political and territorial settlement of post-war Europe. It was understood that the Soviet Union had a legitimate interest in ensuring that the countries along her western and south-western borders should not only come within the USSR's 'sphere of influence', but also be governed by regimes that would be politically at the very least well-disposed to their powerful eastern neighbour. If it is true that Stalin overestimated the degree of latitude he had in interfering in the internal politics of the East European states, it is equally true that the explicitly hostile declarations of some western politicians, as well as Russia's long experience of vulnerability to invasion from the west, made Stalin unwaveringly determined that the military security of the USSR should have absolute priority over the political independence of those countries, some of which had in any case recently fought alongside Hitler. In this way, starting with eastern Germany and Poland, Stalin gradually extended direct Soviet political control over most of Central and Eastern Europe, thereby creating a *cordon sanitaire* or protective barrier of buffer states between the Soviet Union and the West. This was the famous 'Iron Curtain' across Europe, stretching from the Baltic to the Black Sea, about which Winston Churchill thundered in his speech at Fulton, Missouri, in 1946, which has often been interpreted as the West's opening verbal salvo of the Cold War.

In fact there had been more than a whiff of grape-shot about soon after the Yalta conference during an open confrontation in Washington between the new American President, Harry Truman (Roosevelt died in April 1945), and the Soviet Foreign Minister, Stalin's old crony from the Tsaritsyn days, Vyacheslav Molotov. In what one commentator described as 'the language of a Missouri mule-driver', Truman publicly harangued his visiting Soviet ally over what he regarded as the unacceptable composition of the proposed government of Poland, on which a compromise agreement had already been reached at Yalta. There was a heated exchange, but Stalin immediately wrote to the President in remarkably restrained tones pointing out the Soviet Union's crucial interest in ensuring the existence of a friendly government in adjacent Poland, and reminding him, correctly, that the USSR had neither been consulted about, nor claimed the right to interfere in, the establishment of the governments of, for instance, Greece or Belgium in the western sphere. 'To put it plainly', he wrote, 'you want me to renounce the interests of the security of the Soviet Union; but I cannot proceed against the interests of my own country'. Stalin's face-to-face meeting with Truman at the Potsdam conference in July–August 1945 did nothing to dispel the mounting antipathy between the two still formally allied leaders; indeed, it served only to confirm their suspicions about each other's hostile intentions and drive them into even more firmly entrenched positions. Well before Churchill's Iron Curtain speech, therefore, the tone of the Cold War and the bellicose language in which it was to be conducted had been established.

In fact, some of the misinterpretations of each other's actions and intentions in the early stages of the Cold War lay in the imperfect,

Soviet-dominated Eastern Europe 1939–49

0   500
Miles

N

Karelia

FINLAND

NORWAY

SWEDEN

Leningrad

Estonia   USSR

Riga   Latvia

N.E. Prussia Lithuania   to
                                    Moscow ⟶

Belorussia

Berlin
EAST   Warsaw
GERMANY POLAND   E.Poland   Ukraine
     Prague
WEST   CZECHOSLOVAKIA   Ruthenia
GERMANY   N. Bukovina
    AUSTRIA   Budapest   Bessarabia
                          (Moldavia)
ITALY   HUNGARY ROMANIA
     Trieste
        Belgrade   Bucharest
     YUGOSLAVIA   Black Sea

BULGARIA
     Sofia
ALBANIA   Istanbul   TURKEY

═══ Iron curtain	People's Republics established in:
---- International borders	1945 Albania, Yugoslavia
Annexed 1939–40	1946 Bulgaria
Annexed 1944–45	1947 Romania
Soviet-dominated countries 1948	1948 Czechoslovakia, Poland
Red Army stationed	1949 East Germany, Hungary

ambivalent conclusions of the end-of-war conferences. Many of the most contentious issues raised at Teheran, Yalta and Potsdam were deferred, and even when agreements were reached, they tended to be vaguely worded and open to differing interpretations and conflicting inferences. For instance, the concept of 'free elections' meant different things to different people. And, given Russia's experience of what the Soviet leadership regarded as western perfidy, it was obvious that Stalin would give priority to the establishment of 'friendly governments' on its borders, rather than ones elected on the American or British model.

On 6 and 9 August 1945, the United States of America dropped atomic bombs on the Japanese cities of Hiroshima and Nagasaki. It is impossible here to explore the complex web of military, political, moral and technological arguments surrounding Truman's personal decision to use these dreadful new weapons of war, thus making the USA the first, and so far the only, country in the world ever to launch nuclear 'weapons of mass destruction' against an enemy. There is, however, an abundance of evidence to suggest that the decision was motivated as much by political considerations in relation to the Soviet Union as by military objectives against Japan. Even before the bomb was successfully tested, Truman had remarked, with reference to the Russians, *not* the Japanese, 'If it explodes . . . I'll have a hammer on those boys!' The American Secretary of State, James Byrnes, was also quite explicit in his opinion that the United States' possession and demonstration of the bomb 'would make Russia more manageable in Europe'.

He was wrong. If anything, it made Stalin even more intransigent in his determination to strengthen his grip on Eastern Europe. Between 1946 and 1949 communist-dominated puppet governments were systematically imposed on East Germany, Poland, Czechoslovakia, Hungary, Romania and Bulgaria, as the western allies joined the United States in its vigorous campaign to 'contain' the spread of communism across Europe at almost any cost. In the case of Yugoslavia, Marshal Tito's ideological break with Stalin in 1948 suggested that disunity within the Soviet bloc was capable of being encouraged, extended and exploited to Stalin's disadvantage. Despite the Soviet–Yugoslav rift, on the whole the West persisted for many years in seeing communist Eastern Europe as monolithic, with every regime taking orders from the Kremlin as part of a strategy for world domination. Consequently, the so-called 'Truman doctrine' of 'containment' gradually gave way to the policy of 'roll-back' – that is, an attempt to undermine the Soviet Union's monopoly of power in her 'satellite' countries and overthrow their communist governments. Some western statesmen even privately advocated the use of nuclear weapons to bring this about – not so much a policy of 'roll-back' as of 'wipe-out'! Stalin's response was a series of purges, arrests, proscriptions, trials and even executions of East European politicians suspected of anti-Soviet leanings or 'Titoist' sympathies, and to impose his own brand of socialism through terror everywhere east of the river Elbe. It was not any more a policy of building the Stalinist model of 'socialism in one country', but 'socialism in one bloc'.

In 1949 three important events took place. The first was the formation of the North Atlantic Treaty Organization (NATO), a formal alliance of eleven West European and North American powers directed specifically against the Soviet bloc. The second was the successful testing of the atomic bomb by the USSR. In effect, the nuclear arms race was now definitely on the international agenda. And third was the victory of the communist revolution in China and the establishment of the Chinese People's Republic. Although the Soviet Union had played no part in Mao Tse-tung's triumph, the fact that the territorially largest and the demographically most populous countries in the world were now both governed by communist dictatorships added to the alarm of the capitalist powers and their Third World colonial dependencies in Asia and elsewhere. The Cold War had now shifted from being a conflict over spheres of influence in Europe to a global confrontation between two military superpowers and their respective allies, both of them armed, from 1953 onwards, with the hydrogen bomb and both, therefore, with the potential power to plunge the entire planet into a nuclear holocaust.

Although both Stalin and Truman may have misinterpreted each other's military intentions and/or capabilities in the early stages of the Cold War, this is the awesome responsibility they left their political heirs to shoulder when they both, in their different ways, departed from the political scene in 1953.

Death

Stalin's seventieth birthday was celebrated in December 1949 amidst extravagant outpourings of official encomia, obsequious greetings, exhibitions, publications, poetry and even prayers. Apart from the ritual references to the various manifestations of his superlative leadership and genius, the more effusive offerings contained intimations of immortality. But not even Stalin was able to organize that. His mental condition was deteriorating and the last years of his life were spent shuttling between his office in the Kremlin and his country house, or *dacha*, just outside Moscow, surrounded by the members of his Politburo and personal entourage. Stalin worked mainly at night and his subordinates were expected to follow suit. They were also compelled to participate in the regular parties and heavy drinking sessions to which he had become increasingly addicted and which often featured music, dancing, crude practical jokes and drunken horseplay. The picture of Stalin at this time which emerges from Khrushchev's later memoirs is graphically described by their editor as

> the degeneration of this Attila figure into a broken and paranoid old man, scheming to destroy his closest colleagues before they destroyed him, afraid of the food from his own kitchens, but still striking terror into the hearts of all around him.

The most prominent people around him, who were later to form the so-called 'collective leadership' after Stalin's death, were Malenkov, Molotov, Kaganovich, Beria, Khrushchev, Mikoyan and Voroshilov, all of them plotting and scheming in an atmosphere of fear and mutual suspicion. The most senior member of the Politburo after Stalin himself, Andrei Zhdanov, had died, probably of natural causes, in 1948. He was replaced as head of the Leningrad party organization by Giorgii Malenkov, who seemed to be being groomed for the leadership succession. However, his authority was offset to some extent by the recall of Khrushchev from the post-war re-collectivization drive in Ukraine and his appointment as head of the Moscow party organization. Beria, too, had a potentially formidable power base in the NKVD, although the fate of his two predecessors at its head, Yagoda and Yezhov, did not suggest that the position was exactly free of risk. From his Leningrad base, and with Stalin's obvious approval, Malenkov inaugurated a purge of senior party officials and Zhdanov protégés to consolidate his own position. The 'Leningrad Affair', as it came to be known, in fact spread far beyond Leningrad and resulted in the dismissal, arrest and execution of an unknown number of people in the party and government hierarchy. Though nowhere on the same scale as the Great Terror, it was nevertheless an ominous reminder of the sinister methods and mayhem of the 'thirties.

Proximity to Stalin was no guarantee of political survival or personal safety and there is a fair amount of evidence to suggest that around

1952 Stalin was on the verge of another major shake-up of personnel. In October of that year the Communist Party held its 19th Congress, the first for thirteen years. Stalin used the opportunity not only to alter the party statutes but also to disband the tightly knit Politburo and replace it with a much larger, more amorphous policy-making body renamed the Praesidium. This at any rate implied a dilution of the authority of the old Politburo members, which could hardly have increased their sense of well-being. Added to this, some members of Molotov's and Mikoyan's family had been arrested; Stalin's long-serving personal secretary, the shadowy Poskrëbyshev, had been dismissed; and even the odious Beria was under something of a cloud as a result of his mishandling of the affairs of his, and Stalin's, native Georgia. In Eastern Europe, the trials of leading Communist Party officials were going ahead. Then in January 1953 came news of the 'Doctors' Plot'. It was announced that nine Kremlin doctors, most of them Jewish, had been arrested and accused of deliberately bringing about the death of Zhdanov in 1948 and of conspiring to assassinate a number of senior military figures. They were further charged with maintaining links with overseas intelligence agencies and international Jewish organizations. The echoes of the purges of the 1930s were unmistakable.

All the omens seemed to indicate the Stalin was about to launch yet another wave of terror. However, if that was indeed his intention, he was prevented from doing so by the timely intervention of a fatal brain haemorrhage on 2 March 1953. Part-paralysed, incoherent, semi-conscious and stupefied by alcoholic excess, he died three days later. In the official bulletin, it was solemnly announced that 'The heart of the wise leader and teacher of the Communist Party and the Soviet People – Joseph Vissarionovich Stalin – has ceased to beat'. (Speculation that his death may have been the result of other than natural causes is based on very flimsy evidence, which need not be explored here.) In her memoirs, Stalin's daughter, Svetlana Alliluyeva, describes the deathbed scene. Senior party men had gathered at the secret Kuntsevo *dacha* along with family members and household servants. When the final moment came, many of them, she says, including Malenkov, Khrushchev, Kaganovich, other leading acolytes of the Stalin cult and partners in his crimes, shed genuine tears. It is not facetious to suggest that these tears, while genuine enough, may not have been the expression so much of grief, as of relief.

The body lay in state for three days while thousands and thousands filed in a state of shock past the open coffin. The funeral was held in

Red Square, followed by the enshrinement of his chemically embalmed corpse alongside that of Lenin in the mausoleum. In a final, tragic episode, scores of mourning citizens were crushed and trampled to death by the grief-stricken, frenzied crowds, the last victims of the cult of Stalin.

The public obsequies had been presided over by the members of the Praesidium, with eulogies delivered by Molotov, Malenkov and Beria. Whatever sentiments were openly expressed, and whatever their innermost feelings at their master's demise, his successors now jointly faced the formidable task, as his political trustees, of administering the ambiguous and imponderable legacy of Stalin and Stalinism.

7

The ambiguous legacy

Joseph Stalin was General Secretary of the Communist Party of the Soviet Union for thirty-one years (1922–53). Over the next nearly forty years there were six others (Malenkov, Khrushchev, Brezhnev, Andropov, Chernenko and Gorbachev), three dying in office and three ousted by their rivals within the party leadership. During those years an enormous number of changes – economic, social, administrative, technological, cultural and military – were introduced. The sum total of those changes is often described as a process of *de-Stalinization*; in other words, an undoing, dismantling or reconstruction of the system and the machinery for running it, which Stalin had created. Before discussing to what extent the term is accurate or even appropriate, it is first necessary to define what is meant by Stalinism itself.

Stalinism

In his analysis of the origins and consequences of Stalinism, the Russian Marxist historian Roy Medvedev tells us that he chose the title of his book, *Let History Judge*, as an indication of the inchoate nature of the proper, academic investigation of the Stalin cult, particularly in the Soviet Union where it took place. That was nearly forty years ago, in 1968. Despite mountains of affidavits, accusations, eyewitness accounts and material exhibits, the court of history has not yet pronounced its final verdict, although more and more evidence is coming to light on which a better-informed, objective and ideologically untrammelled judgement may one day be passed. It is, however, possible to identify a number of the specific features of Stalinism, which, when fitted together, produce a kind of imperfect, identikit picture of a unique phenomenon.

First and foremost, there is the 'command economy' and the emphasis on heavy industry. From the inauguration of the first five-year plan and the collectivization of agriculture, every single aspect of economic life and financial activity in the Soviet Union was controlled, or at any rate was *supposed* to be controlled, by the state. This is not just a matter of setting production targets or working out an annual budget. Even in free-enterprise economies, it is ultimately the government that controls fiscal policies and also decides on such things as whether industries and public services should be nationally or privately owned, whether students should receive grants or loans and patients pay for medical treatment. To that extent, central direction of economic priorities is also a feature of capitalist economies. Under the Stalinist-type command economy, however, the state planning authorities and the various centralized ministries were theoretically in charge of the *entire* economic system, from deciding the size of the national defence budget and industrial investment priorities to establishing wage levels, prices, rents, bus fares, food subsidies, pensions, kindergarten fees and funeral expenses. There were no such things as private banks, commercial advertising, stocks and shares, insurance firms or limited companies. A small amount of private trade was legally tolerated – for instance, collective farmers could sell the produce grown on their personal allotments at the local market – but even this facility was at the discretion of the state and could therefore be curtailed, extended or withdrawn by the government authorities. Thus, although the *kolkhozniki* were not technically state employees, they were nevertheless subject to central direction and state control. There was, of course, a huge black market, without which, it has been suggested, the command economy simply would not work; indeed, to some extent it even relied on its illegal operation, in the same way that parasites are often essential to the health of the body that hosts them. In addition, there was also a good deal of large-scale organized crime. Otherwise, everyone, from Communist Party official to circus clown, was an employee of the state.

The second, and in a sense perhaps most glaringly obvious, feature of the system is what Khrushchev described as the 'cult of personality'; that is, the elevation of one person, his transformation into a super-man possessing supernatural characteristics, akin to those of a god. Such a man supposedly knows everything, sees every-thing, thinks for everyone, can do anything, is infallible in his behaviour.

'Such a belief about Stalin', continues Khrushchev, 'was cultivated among us for many years'. Enough has already been said in the preceding pages to give an idea of the extraordinary, unprecedented proportions of the Stalin cult during his own lifetime. Two quotations will suffice here to illustrate the absurd nature of the adulation heaped upon him. The first is from Alexander Solzhenitsyn's novel *The First Circle*:

His image, more than any other human likeness in history, had been graven in stone, painted in oils, in water colour, in gouache and in sepia, drawn in charcoal, chalk and brickdust, patterned in gravel, seashells, glazed tiles, grains of wheat and soya beans, carved in ivory, grown in grass, woven in carpets, registered on celluloid and outlined in the sky by planes.

The second is a poem, or hymn, published in *Pravda* in 1936:

O great Stalin, O leader of the peoples,
Thou who broughtest man to birth,
Thou who fructifiest the earth,
Thou who restorest the centuries,
Thou who makest bloom the spring,
Thou who makest vibrate the chords of music . . .
Thou, splendour of my spring, O Thou,
Sun reflected by millions of hearts . . .

The patent absurdity of these grovelling paeans has only been matched in modern times by the inane adulation heaped on Mao Tse-tung at the height of China's 'Cultural Revolution' during the 1960s.

The third, and most sinister, feature is the operation of the police state and the implementation of rule by terror. Again, earlier chapters have referred to the various manifestations of NKVD activity with which Stalin maintained his tyrannical rule. Russia has a long, dreadful tradition of police or quasi-police enforcement of government policy stretching way back to the times of Ivan the Terrible (r. 1533–84), who literally split his kingdom in two with the creation of the *oprichnina*, a kind of state within a state, whose dreaded agents – the *oprichniki* – terrorized the rest of the population in an orgy of pillage, rape and murder. Later on, Peter the Great (r. 1682–1725) introduced his own peculiar reign of terror to coerce the population into implementing his supposedly civilizing, European-style reforms. This, as often noted, was an exercise in 'driving out barbarism with the use of barbaric methods'. In the nineteenth century, Nicholas I (r. 1825–55) and Alexander III (r. 1881–94) were the two emperors most closely identified with the reliance on 'secret police' organizations to maintain their oppressive and reactionary regimes. Nicholas's 'Third Section' and Alexander's *Okhrana* (the undercover wing of the Police Department) were clear prototypes of the twentieth-century *Cheka*, OGPU, NKVD and the more recent KGB (see Glossary). Although the mind-set and the methods used by their predecessors were similar, Stalin and his agents sank to lower, but greater, levels of mass intimidation. The whole ghastly business of denunciation, arrest, interrogation, torture, imprisonment, exile, concentration camps and executions to which millions fell victim under Stalin was an indispensable element of his system of political coercion and social control.

However, despite its monstrous proportions, the police apparatus was unable to impose and maintain absolutely total control over the entire population of the largest country in the world. Despite the use of (pre-computer-age) modern technology and means of communication and surveillance, the Orwellian image of the all-seeing, all-knowing 'Big Brother' state was never fully realized. As millions were netted in the deadly trawl, so millions more continued with their hum-drum affairs and daily preoccupations without ever seeing the inside of a prison cell or a barbed-wire encampment.

Fourth, there is what might be called the 'mobilized society'. This is something we are familiar with in times of total war, when not only the armed forces but every section of society is geared in some way towards the achievement of a common national goal – in this case the defeat of the enemy. Under Stalinism, in peacetime and in war, each individual citizen of the Soviet Union was recruited, educated, trained, exhorted, regimented and, ultimately, coerced into carrying out his or her patriotic/political duty in the great historical task of building socialism and marching under Stalin's banner towards the inevitable victory of communism. This was not just a matter of fulfilling one's work norm at the factory, farm or office. One's entire life-style was conditioned by the policies of the Party and the leviathan state. Independent clubs, associations and non-official unions were proscribed and persecuted out of existence. The Church was crushed. Even people's leisure time activities were meant to have a place and a purpose in Stalin's grand plan. Public or anonymous denunciations of suspected 'deviationists' were common, and even schoolchildren were encouraged to report to the authorities members of their family, their own parents, if they heard disloyal or critical opinions voiced in the dubious privacy of the home.

A notorious example of the latter is the case of Pavlik Morozov in 1932. Pavlik was a 14-year-old youth who – so the story goes – denounced his own father for some kind of petty crime or fraud, and was killed for his action by his uncle. The boy was given the full posthumous propaganda treatment as a paragon of socialist virtue and turned into a kind of folk hero. (Despite the notoriety of the tale, its total authenticity has been recently called into question, though it is genuinely symptomatic of the atmosphere of suspicion and recrimination prevalent at the time.) The terrifyingly indiscriminate nature of the whole whistle-blowing campaign is also illustrated by the following anecdote:

> Three inmates of a Siberian labour-camp were talking together:
> *1ˢᵗ inmate:* 'What are you in for?'
> *2ⁿᵈ inmate:* 'I denounced Ivanov. How about you?'
> *1ˢᵗ inmate:* 'I made a speech in defence of Ivanov.'
> They then asked the third inmate: 'And you?'
> *3ʳᵈ inmate:* 'Me? I'm Ivanov.'

Stalinism also sought to mobilize not just the bodies but also the minds of the population. This was not just a case of toeing the party line on ideological or policy issues. It involved the whole apparatus of propaganda, literary censorship of everything written and printed – from scientific treatises to tram-tickets – political control of education, research and scholarship and a total ban on all manifestations of intellectual individualism, heterodoxy or dissent. Cultural standardization and uniformity was imposed not just on creative literature, but also on painting, music, theatre, ballet and even architecture – the great leader favouring the gigantic monstrosities of the so-called 'Stalin-baroque' style, of which the Hotel Ukraine and the central building of Moscow State University are prime examples.

Finally, although the list is not exhaustive, a characteristic feature of Stalinism, which it shares with other examples of totalitarianism, is its rampant nationalism. The emphasis on the people, 'the folk', on race and Soviet patriotism – barely distinguishable from the tsarist brand of 'Great Russian' nationalism – went far beyond simple love of country. In gross distortion of the internationalist principles of original Marxism and Leninism, it took on the most unsavoury and obnoxious features of chauvinism, racial discrimination, a crude contempt for other cultural values, and a dangerous xenophobia that for a while made even talking to foreigners a criminal offence. The devastating impact of such odious policies on the non-Russian peoples of the Soviet union has already been alluded to in Chapter 4.

Some of these features of Stalinism (and, to repeat, they do not form an exhaustive list) can be found to a greater or lesser extent in other examples of totalitarian regimes. Hitler's Germany, Mussolini's Italy, Mao's China, Pol-Pot's Kampuchea and Pinochet's Chile are cases in point, but the peculiar and perverse blend in which they were experienced in Stalin's USSR makes his a distressingly unique and, one hopes, unrepeatable model.

De-Stalinization

Very soon after the dictator's death, various component parts of his system were subjected to a number of uncoordinated modifications and reforms that attenuated some of its harsher aspects. The universally detested Beria was arrested and summarily shot, and the recently renamed KGB (Committee for State Security) placed firmly under party control. So far as we know, Beria's was the last political execution to have taken place in the Soviet Union. (So determined was the new leadership to have him 'unpersoned' that even overseas subscribers to the *Great Soviet Encyclopaedia* were sent instructions to cut out his extensive biographical entry in volume 5, and replace it with a new set of pages containing an extended article on the Bering Strait!) In domestic policies a greater emphasis was given to the manufacture of consumer goods, an extensive housing programme was launched, collective farmers were granted more concessions and incentives, and the first, faint stirrings of a cultural 'thaw' began to be felt. Many of the purge victims who had managed to stay alive were released from the camps and began to pick up the pieces of their shattered lives.

In the realm of foreign policy there was a shift away from an insistence on the inevitability of military confrontation between capitalism and socialism and a revival of the old Leninist principle of 'peaceful co-existence'. Comradely overtures were made to Tito's Yugoslavia, and the Soviet government and party leaders Bulganin and Khrushchev (known to the west as 'B & K') embarked on a series of visits to capitalist countries (including Britain), something that Stalin had never done. When he was in power, the rotund, almost jovial figure of Nikita Khrushchev, with his bald pate, gap-toothed grin and earthy – sometimes vulgar – peasant humour, became a well-known and regular performer on the international stage. Commercial, cultural and academic links contributed to the steady relaxation of international tension, despite such danger points as the building of the Berlin Wall in 1961 and the Cuban missile crisis in 1962.

Back in the mid-1950s, there was still no actual official policy that was called 'de-Stalinization' and no public acknowledgement that there was to be any radical departure from established procedures and attitudes. But then, in 1956, Khrushchev dropped a bombshell among the ranks of the party faithful. At the 20th Party Congress he delivered his famous 'secret speech' in which he attacked the 'cult of personality' and informed his dumbstruck audience that, far from being the wise and beneficent object of their earlier adulation, Stalin was in fact a bloodthirsty, criminal tyrant who had trampled on Leninist principles, overthrown standards of socialist legality, and sent thousands of innocent party comrades to their doom. It is difficult to convey the full impact of Khrushchev's dramatic revelations, but the shock-waves reverberated throughout the Party, the country, the Eastern bloc and the world communist movement. It was rather as if a Pope had denied the Virgin Birth and Resurrection, and officially declared to a Vatican Council that Jesus Christ was not the Son of God but a murderer, a charlatan and a crook.

At any rate the 'secret speech' was a major turning point in the history of the Soviet Union and led to a spate of liberalizing policies and intensified reforms. In Eastern Europe, Khrushchev's excori-ation of Stalin led to unlooked-for consequences as the people of Hungary misinterpreted his speech as signalling a slackening of Soviet domination of their country. When the Hungarian leader, Imre Nagy, threatened to withdraw his country from the Warsaw Pact, Khrushchev reasserted Soviet control and crushed the Hungarian upris-ing with Russian tanks. Nagy himself was executed in 1958. Despite this blatantly Stalinist manoeuvre, at home in Russia Stalin himself was subjected to the same process of 'depersonification' as his previous victims, and his name all but eradicated from the textbooks. Stalingrad, scene of his greatest military triumph, was renamed Volgograd, and in 1961 his body was unceremoniously removed from Lenin's side in the mausoleum and buried near the Kremlin wall. (Rumour has it that, as a precautionary measure, the coffin was covered with thick, solid concrete!) Khrushchev even suggested that there should be an official commission of inquiry into Stalin's crimes and a public monument to his victims, though nothing came of it. After all, too many high-ranking party officials had good reason for wishing to avoid too much public muck-raking, including Khrushchev himself.

De-Stalinization was an ambiguous process. It was being implemented, after all, by men who had made their careers out of blindly obeying his will. Veteran, died-in-the-wool Stalinists were attempting to dismantle Stalinism without bringing down the whole edifice that they had helped to build. There were in any case many still around in powerful positions who thought things had already gone far enough, or even too far, in the direction of liberalization and reform. In 1964 Khrushchev was himself ousted from office and succeeded by a team of unimaginative senior *apparatchiki* headed by Leonid Brezhnev (1906–82), who presided over almost two decades of economic and cultural immobility (or stability?), which were later officially condemned as the 'era of stagnation'. This was in contrast to the uncertain, oscillating policies and mercurial temperament of Khrushchev, whose sudden initiatives, U-turns and 'hare-brained scheming' had alienated some of his more cautious and conservative-minded comrades on the Politburo. Khrushchev's famous secret speech was never published, and though Stalin was *not* formally rehabilitated, his heinous crimes were conveniently and euphemistically glossed over as 'errors', 'deviations from Leninist norms', or 'consequences of the personality cult'. In 1969, the ninetieth anniversary of his birth was marked by a long, fairly anodyne article in the party newspaper *Pravda*, and behind the mausoleum a plinth, surmounted with his bust, was raised above his gravestone.

Dissident intellectuals and critics, writers who circulated uncensored literature or published it abroad, 'anti-Soviet agitators', religious activists and would-be emigrant Jews were subjected to a sustained campaign of official harassment and police persecution. This often led to the public trial, imprisonment, confinement in psychiatric units, exile or banishment of those whose only alleged crime was to call attention to what they saw as the threat of a possible return to the standards and practices of the Stalin period. The two best-known luminaries of the dissident movement were the novelist and Nobel laureate, Alexander Solzhenitsyn, who was forcibly expelled from the Soviet Union in 1974, and the renowned nuclear physicist and human rights activist, Andrei Sakharov. Also a Nobel prize-winner, for Peace (1975), Sakharov was sent to live under virtual house arrest in the provincial town of Gorky, hundreds of miles from Moscow.

Despite the atmosphere of 'stagnation', inertia and lack of vigour on the part of the increasingly geriatric party leadership, the dissidents, protesters and oppositionists had reason for disquiet. In 1968, Soviet troops invaded Czechoslovakia and, in a grim repeat of the events in Hungary twelve years before, brutally extinguished the reform movement led by Alexander Dubček during the 'Prague Spring'. During the 'seventies and early 'eighties, in terms of the various 'ingredients' of Stalinism discussed in the previous section, apart from the excesses of the cult of personality itself, there was still plenty of evidence of the command economy, the powers of the many-tentacled KGB, the mobilization of human resources in the interests of the state, a rather limited cultural scene (though there were some major scientific achievements), and intense national chauvinism. The bloodletting of the Great Terror was absent, but a powerful residue still remained of die-hard attitudes and institutions, behavioural patterns, economic and military priorities, and knee-jerk responses to external stimuli that were all part of the brainwashed, conditioned-reflex system of 'classical' Stalinism, and which did so much to undermine Gorbachev's attempts to reform the system.

Glasnost and after

When the first edition of this pamphlet was written in 1989, it was less than half a decade since Mikhail Gorbachev had taken over the post of Communist Party General Secretary, the position which Stalin had made so powerful. In those few years a tremendous sea-change occurred in the Soviet Union, on which it was then too soon for a historian to pass proper judgement. However, many of the ripples originally set in motion by Khrushchev's attack on the cult of personality, and which then disappeared during the years of Brezhnevite stagnation, began to billow and surge once more with a renewed force, eventually creating a tidal wave that swept away the post-Stalinist regime and the USSR with it. Ancient taboos had been broken, old outcasts and opponents were officially rehabilitated, and skeletons hidden in the gloomy cupboard of Soviet history were brought out into the light of public debate and academic scrutiny.

More tragically and dramatically, real skeletons of thousands of Stalin's victims were discovered and unearthed from mass graves in Belorussia, Ukraine, Siberia and elsewhere. Surviving eyewitnesses revealed to the press their memories of the long nights of terror as the forests reverberated with the continuous sound of NKVD gunfire, and there were public calls for the perpetrators of those horrors who were still alive to be hunted down and tried in the same way as Nazi war criminals. In Moscow, an officially approved organization called Memorial, funded by public donation and bequest, was established to investigate the crimes of Stalin and to raise a monument to the memory of his victims. There were candlelit protest vigils around the notorious Lubyanka prison and headquarters of the KGB in central Moscow. Those who had not, could not, or dared not speak out in the past suddenly enjoyed the opportunities of *glasnost* to pursue their investigations in the full glare of publicity. The works of foreign scholars who had written of the Stalinist past and had been vilified for their books were now openly published and their authors fêted in newspaper columns and the lecture theatres of Soviet universities. In 1988 Nikolai Bukharin was formally rehabilitated by a judicial enquiry and posthumously restored to party membership, apparently a great source of comfort to his surviving widow. The economic tracts of this major champion of NEP and victim of Stalin's terror appeared on public sale, and it even became possible to read dispassionate articles and books discussing the historical role of erstwhile arch enemy, Trotsky, in terms that would not, until then, have been contemplated. Critical biographies of Stalin and disparaging articles analysing his regime proliferated.

At a meeting of the party Central Committee in 1989, Gorbachev himself roundly condemned the atrocities committed in Stalin's drive to collectivize the peasantry in the 1930s, and used his authority to exhort writers and historians to fill in the 'blank pages' in Russia's recent past – pages on which their predecessors were too craven, ignorant or obsequious to write. Not even the once sacrosanct figure of Lenin escaped the new revisionism and iconoclasm sweeping through the Russian historiography of the country's past. Visual symbols of that past have been destroyed, and the statues of disgraced, detested historical figures and emblems of the darker side of Soviet history have been toppled from their pedestals. They now lie, shattered and muti-lated, in their own grotesque 'graveyard' near Moscow's Gorky Park.

Since Gorbachev, the architect of *glasnost*, was removed from office amid the débâcle of the Soviet Union in 1991, the Russian Federation has travelled a path of post-communist nation-building that has been fraught with difficulty, danger and uncertainty. The transition from a one-party state to a dodgy democracy, from a command economy to an imperfect market system and inchoate capitalism, and from super-power status to a position of comparatively limited international clout, has been both a liberating and a humiliating experience. Some of the problems with which President Putin and his government have to grapple are referred to in the preface to this book. How they will cope with them has yet to be seen, but in strengthening the Russian state and its economy, in regaining international prestige, and in trying to heal the nation's social lesions, the temptations of reverting to authoritarian practices must be eschewed.

Following Putin's overwhelming, if flawed, success in the 2004 elections, a British newspaper headline suggested that the re-elected president now enjoys all the powers that Stalin once possessed, backed up by a popular mandate. This is obviously to overstate the situation. However, extreme nationalism and a dubious nostalgia for the dis-cipline, patriotic pride and certainties of the Stalin years still remain among certain sections of Russian society. Stalin's portraits are still occasionally to be seen displayed in public demonstrations. Unrecon-stituted Communists still remain a force on the political scene and in the Russian parliament. Even Putin has restored the tune, though not the words, of the old Stalinist state anthem. Nevertheless, it does appear that the malign spirit of Joseph Vissarionovich Stalin, which continued to haunt the Soviet Union long after his death, has finally been cast out. It remains to be seen whether the exorcism has been permanently successful, or whether the ghost will return.

Suggestions for further reading

The English-language literature on Stalin is enormous in quantity and varied in quality. What follows is a brief, highly selective list, arranged by sections which are part thematic and part chronological in order, of some of the more interesting, respectable and in some cases controversial works on Stalin, Stalinism and the Stalinist period of Soviet history. To accompany a book of this limited size and scope, the list cannot even pretend to be comprehensive, and the author is of course aware that other writers might have included other material. However, most of the following suggestions contain extensive notes and bibliographical references which the reader may consult for more extensive guidance.

References

Brown, A., Fennell, J., Kaser, M. and Willetts, H. (eds.), *The Cambridge Encyclopedia of Russia and the Soviet Union*, Cambridge: Cambridge University Press, 1982.

Channon, J. and Hudson, R., *The Penguin Atlas of Russia*, Harmondsworth: Penguin, 1995.

McCauley, M., *Who's Who in Russia Since 1900*, London: Routledge, 1997.

Vronskaya, J., *A Biographical Dictionary of the Soviet Union 1917–1988*, London: K. G. Saur, 1989.

Documents

Andrews, W. G. (ed.), *Soviet Institutions and Policies: Inside Views*, Princeton, NJ: Van Nostrand, 1966.

McCauley, M. (ed.), *The Russian Revolution and the Soviet State, 1917–1921: Documents*, Basingstoke: Macmillan, 1975.

McNeal, R. (ed.), *Resolutions and Decisions of the Communist Party of the Soviet Union* (Vol. 3), Toronto: Toronto University Press, 1974.

Murphy, A. B. (ed.), *The Russian Civil War: Primary Sources*, New York: St Martin's Press, 2000.

Riha, T. (ed.), *Readings in Russian Civilization* (3 vols. in one), Chicago, IL: University of Chicago Press, 1964.

Stalin, J. V., *Collected Works*, 13 vols., Moscow: Foreign Languages Publishing House, 1952–55.

Suny, R. G. (ed.), *The Structure of Soviet History: Essays and Documents*, Oxford: Oxford University Press, 2003.

Memoirs

Alliluyeva, S., *Twenty Letters to a Friend*, Harmondsworth: Penguin, 1967.

Djilas, M., *Conversations with Stalin*, Harmondsworth: Penguin, 1963.

Ginzburg, E., *Into the Whirlwind*, Harmondsworth: Penguin, 1968.

Khrushchev, N. S., *Khrushchev Remembers*, London: Andre Deutsch, 1971.

Khrushchev, N. S., *Khrushchev Remembers: The Last Testament*, London: Andre Deutsch, 1974.

Kravchenko, V., *I Chose Freedom*, London: Robert Hale, 1947.

Mandelstam, N., *Hope Against Hope*, Harmondsworth: Penguin, 1975.

Mandelstam, N., *Hope Abandoned*, Harmondsworth: Penguin, 1979.

Molotov, V., *Molotov Remembers: Inside Kremlin Politics*, Chicago, IL: University of Chicago Press, 1993.

Serge, V., *Memoirs of a Revolutionary, 1901–1941*, Oxford: Oxford University Press, 1963.

Trotsky, L., *My Life: An Attempt at an Autobiography*, Harmondsworth: Penguin, 1975.

General histories of the USSR

Hosking, G., *A History of the Soviet Union, 1917–1991* (final edn.), London: Fontana Press, 1992.

Hough, J. and Fainsod, M., *How the Soviet Union is Governed*, Cambridge, MA: Harvard University Press, 1979.

Kenez, P., *A History of the Soviet Union from the Beginning to its End*, Cambridge: Cambridge University Press, 1999.

McCauley, M., *The Soviet Union, 1917–1991* (2nd edn.), London: Longman, 1993.

Nove, A., *An Economic History of the USSR*, Harmondsworth: Penguin, 1986.

Service, R., *A History of Twentieth-Century Russia*, Harmondsworth: Penguin, 1998.

The Communist Party of the Soviet Union

Commission of the Central Committee of the CPSU[B] (eds.), *History of the Communist Party of the Soviet Union [Bolsheviks]*, Moscow: Foreign Languages Publishing House, 1939.

Hill, R. J. and Frank, P., *The Soviet Communist Party*, London: Allen & Unwin, 1981.

Hough, J. and Fainsod, M., *How the Soviet Union is Governed*, Cambridge, MA: Harvard University Press, 1979.

Schapiro, L., *The Communist Party of the Soviet Union* (2nd edn.), London: Eyre & Spottiswoode, 1970.

Biographies (i): Stalin

Carrère d'Encausse, H., *Stalin: Order through Terror*, London: Longman, 1981.

Deutscher, I., *Stalin: A Political Biography* (revised edn.), Harmondsworth: Penguin, 1966.

Laqueur, W., *Stalin: The Glasnost Revelations*, London: Unwin Hyman, 1990.

McNeal, R. H., *Stalin: Man and Ruler*, Basingstoke: Macmillan, 1988.

Montefiore, S. S., *Stalin: The Court of the Red Tsar*, London: Weidenfeld & Nicolson, 2003.

Rayfield, D., *Stalin and his Hangmen*, London: Viking/Penguin, 2004.

Souvarine, *Stalin*, London: Secker & Warburg, 1939.

Volkogonov, D., *Stalin: Triumph and Tragedy*, London: Weidenfeld & Nicolson, 1991.

Stalinism

Fitzpatrick, S. (ed.), *Stalinism: New Directions*, London: Routledge, 2000.

Hoffman, D. L. (ed.), *Stalinism: The Essential Readings*, Oxford: Blackwell, 2003.

Mawdsley, E., *The Stalin Years: The Soviet Union, 1929–1953*, Manchester: Manchester University Press, 1998.

Medvedev, R. A., *On Stalin and Stalinism*, Oxford: Oxford University Press, 1979.

Nove, A., *Stalinism and After* (3rd edn.), London: Unwin Hyman, 1989.

Read, C., *The Stalin Years: A Reader*, Basingstoke: Palgrave Macmillan, 2003.

Tucker, R. C. (ed.), *Stalinism: Essays in Historical Interpretation*, New York: Norton, 1977.

Ward, C. (ed.), *The Stalinist Dictatorship*, London: Arnold, 1998.

Ward, C., *Stalin's Russia* (2nd edn.), London: Arnold, 1999.

Biographies (ii): other personalities

Volkogonov, D., *The Rise and Fall of the Soviet Empire: Political Leaders from Lenin to Gorbachev*, London: HarperCollins, 1998.

Beria

Beria, S., *Beria, My Father: Inside Stalin's Kremlin*, London: Duckworth, 2001.

Knight, A., *Beria: Stalin's First Lieutenant*, Princeton, NJ: Princeton University Press, 1993.

Bukharin

Cohen, S., *Bukharin and the Bolshevik Revolution: A Political Biography*, London: Wildwood House, 1973.

Katkov, G., *The Trial of Bukharin*, London: Batsford, 1969.

Khrushchev

Crankshaw, E., *Khrushchev: A Biography*, London: Heron Books, 1966.

Medvedev, R. and Medvedev, Zh., *Khrushchev: The Years in Power*, Oxford: Oxford University Press, 1977.

Medvedev, R., *Khrushchev*, Oxford: Blackwell, 1982.

Lenin

Service, R., *Lenin: A Biography*, Basingstoke: Macmillan, 2000.
Volkogonov, D., *Lenin: Life and Legacy*, London: HarperCollins, 1995.

Trotsky

Deutscher, I., *The Prophet Armed: Trotsky, 1879–1921*, Oxford: Oxford University Press, 1954.
Deutscher, I., *The Prophet Unarmed: Trotsky, 1921–1929*, Oxford: Oxford University Press, 1959.
Deutscher, I., *The Prophet Outcast: Trotsky, 1921–1940*, Oxford: Oxford University Press, 1980.

Vyshinsky

Vaksberg, A., *The Prosecutor and the Prey: Vyshinsky and the 1930s Moscow Show Trials*, London: Weidenfeld & Nicolson, 1990.

Zhukov

Chaney, O. P., *Zhukov*, Norman, OK: University of Oklahoma Press, 1971.

1917 Revolution and Civil War

Figes, O., *A People's Tragedy: The Russian Revolution, 1891–1924*, London: Jonathan Cape, 1996.
Fitzpatrick, S., *The Russian Revolution, 1917–32*, Oxford: Oxford University Press, 1982.
Mawdsley, E., *The Russian Civil War*, London: Allen & Unwin, 1987.
Pipes, R., *The Russian Revolution, 1899–1919*, London: Fontana Press, 1990.
Pipes, R., *The Bolsheviks in Power, 1919–1924*, London: Harper-Collins, 1994.
Service, R., *The Russian Revolution, 1900–1927* (3rd edn.), Basingstoke: Macmillan, 1999.
Trotsky, L., *History of the Russian Revolution* (3 vols.), London: Sphere Books, reprinted 1967.
Wood, A., *The Origins of the Russian Revolution, 1861–1917* (3rd edn.), London: Routledge, 2003.

The 1920s

Brovkin, V., *Russia after Lenin: Politics, Culture and Society, 1921–1929*, London: Routledge, 1998.

Carr, E. H., *The Interregnum, 1924–1926* (2 vols.), Basingstoke: Macmillan, 1958–59.

Deutscher, I., *The Prophet Unarmed: Trotsky, 1921–1929*, Oxford: Oxford University Press, 1959.

Fainsod, M., *Smolensk Under Soviet Rule*, Basingstoke: Macmillan, 1958.

Gill, G., *The Origins of the Stalinist Political System*, Cambridge: Cambridge University Press, 1990.

Hughes, J., *Stalin, Siberia and the Crisis of the New Economic Policy*, Cambridge: Cambridge University Press, 1991.

Kenez, P., *The Birth of the Propaganda State: Soviet Methods of Mass Mobilization*, Cambridge: Cambridge University Press, 1985.

Lewin, M., *Lenin's Last Struggle*, London: Faber & Faber, 1969.

Pethybridge, R., *The Social Prelude to Stalinism*, Basingstoke: Macmillan, 1974.

Collectivization and industrialization

Davies, R. W., *The Industrialization of Soviet Russia* (6 vols.), Basingstoke: Macmillan, 1980–96.

Goldman, W. Z., *Women at the Gates: Gender and Industry in Stalin's Russia*, Cambridge: Cambridge University Press, 2002.

Hughes, J., *Stalinism in a Russian Province: Collectivization and Dekulakization in Siberia*, Basingstoke: Macmillan, 1996.

Lewin, M., *Russian Peasants and Soviet Power: A Study of Collectivization*, London: Allen & Unwin, 1968.

Lewin, M., *The Making of the Soviet System: Essays in the Social History of Interwar Russia*, London: Methuen, 1985.

'The Great Terror'

Applebaum, A., *Gulag: A History of the Soviet Camps*, London: Allen Lane/Penguin, 2003.

Conquest, R., *The Great Terror: A Reassessment*, Oxford: Oxford University Press, 1990.

Getty, J. A., *The Origins of the Great Purges: The Soviet Communist Party Reconsidered*, Cambridge: Cambridge University Press, 1986.

Getty, J. A. and Manning, R., *Stalinist Terror: New Perspectives*, Cambridge: Cambridge University Press, 1993.

Getty, J. A. and Naumov, O. (eds.), *The Road to Terror: Stalin and the Self-Destruction of the Bolsheviks, 1932–1939*, New Haven, CT: Yale University Press, 1999.

Medvedev, R., *Let History Judge: The Origins and Consequences of Stalinism*, New York: Knopf, 1971.

Pohl, J. O., *The Stalinist Penal System: A Statistical History of Soviet Repression and Terror, 1930–1953*, Jefferson City, MO: McFarland & Company, 1997.

Rittersporn, G. T., *Stalinist Simplifications and Soviet Complications: Social Tensions and Political Conflict in the USSR, 1933–53*, Reading: Harwood Academic, 1991.

Solzhenitsyn, A., *The Gulag Archipelago* (3 vols.), London: Collins/ Harvill, 1974–78.

Thurston, R. W., *Life and Terror in Stalin's Russia, 1934–1941*, New Haven, CT: Yale University Press, 1996.

Trotsky, L., *The Revolution Betrayed*, London: Faber & Faber, 1937.

[One may also read with profit Arthur Koestler's brilliant novel *Darkness at Noon*, London: Jonathan Cape, 1940 (republished by Penguin Books, 1965).]

The Great Patriotic War

Barber, J. D. and Harrison, M., *The Soviet Home Front: 1941–1945: A Social and Economic History of the USSR in World War II*, London: Longman, 1991.

Beevor, A., *Stalingrad*, Harmondsworth: Penguin, 1999.

Beevor, A., *Berlin: The Downfall, 1945*, Harmondsworth: Penguin, 2003.

Erickson, J., *The Road to Stalingrad*, London: Weidenfeld & Nicolson, 1975.

Erickson, J., *The Road to Berlin*, London: Weidenfeld & Nicolson, 1983.

Glantz, D., *The Siege of Leningrad: 900 Days of Terror*, London: Brown Partworks, 2001.

Glantz, D. and House, J., *When Titans Clashed*, Lawrence, KA: University Press of Kansas, 1995.

Overy, R., *Russia's War*, Harmondsworth: Penguin, 1999.

Roberts, G., *The Soviet Union and the Origins of the Second World War: Russo-German Relations and the Road to War, 1933–1941*, Basingstoke: Macmillan, 1995.

Werth, A., *Russia at War, 1941–1945*, London: Barrie & Rockliffe, 1964.

Stalin's last years and the Cold War

Dunmore, T., *The Stalinist Command Economy: The Soviet State Apparatus and Economic Policy, 1945–53*, Basingstoke, Macmillan, 1980.

Dunmore, T., *Soviet Politics, 1945–53*, Basingstoke: Macmillan, 1984.

Fetjö, F., *A History of the People's Democracies: Eastern Europe since Stalin* (2nd edn.), Harmondsworth: Penguin, 1974.

Hahn, W. G., *Postwar Soviet Politics: The Fall of Zhdanov and the Defeat of Moderation, 1946–53*, Ithaca, NY: Cornell University Press, 1982.

Holloway, D., *Stalin and the Bomb*, New Haven, CT: Yale University Press, 1994.

Joravsky, D., *The Lysenko Affair*, Cambridge, MA: Harvard University Press, 1970.

Linz, S. J. (ed.), *The Impact of World War II on the Soviet Union*, Totowa, NJ: Rowman & Allenheld, 1985.

Mastny, V., *Russia's Road to the Cold War*, New York: Columbia University Press, 1979.

Pethybridge, R., *A History of Post-War Russia*, London: Allen & Unwin, 1966.

Walker, M., *The Cold War*, London: Fourth Estate, 1993.

De-Stalinization and after

Brown, A. and Kaser, M. (eds.), *The Soviet Union Since the Fall of Khrushchev*, London: Macmillan, 1975.

Davies, R. W., *Soviet History in the Gorbachev Revolution*, Basingstoke: Macmillan, 1989.

Davies, R. W., *Soviet History in the Yeltsin Era*, Basingstoke: Macmillan, 1997.

Gorbachev, M., *Perestroika: New Thinking for our Country and the World*, London: Collins, 1987.

Khrushchev, N., *Khrushchev Remembers*, London: Andre Deutsch, 1971 (contains text of Khrushchev's 'secret speech' at the 20th Party Congress, 1956).

Nove, A., *Stalinism and After* (3rd edn.), London: Unwin Hyman, 1989.

Tatu, M., *Power in the Kremlin*, London: Collins, 1968.

[See also the anthologies of essays on Stalinism and post-Stalinism listed in the section above, **Stalinism**.]

Glossary of Russian technical terms and abbreviations

apparat	Soviet party or government bureaucracy
apparatchik	a party or government functionary; member of the *apparat*
Bolshevik	originally, a member of Lenin's 'hard-line' faction of the RSDRP
cadres	full-time professional party activists
Cheka	Extraordinary Commission for Struggle with Counter-revolution and Sabotage, established in 1917, the first Soviet political police
Comintern	Third (Communist) International, established in 1919, dissolved in 1943
dacha	a Russian country house
Duma	elected state assembly with severely limited constitutional powers, 1906–17
Gensec	abbreviation of 'General Secretary'
glasnost	'openness' or 'publicity'; public access to information
GULag	Main Prison Camp Administration
intelligentsia	in Soviet usage, professionally qualified cultural and scientific workers
internat	boarding school for all nationalities of the USSR in which the teaching medium is Russian
KGB	Committee for State Security
Khan	Mongol chieftain
kolkhoz (nik)	collective farm(er)

kulak	a 'rich' peasant (NB: a very elastic term, used in the 1930s to denote peasants who opposed collectivization)
Menshevik	member of the moderate faction of the RSDRP
Messame Dassy	(Georgian) 'The Third Group', a Marxist revolutionary circle in Georgia, joined by Stalin
MTS	Machine Tractor Station; state-controlled supplier of agricultural machinery to collective farms
NEP	New Economic Policy; limited free-market economy operating during 1920s
Nepmen	private entrepreneurs active during NEP
NKVD	People's Commissariat for Internal Affairs, the 'ministry' responsible for Stalin's secret-police operations
okhrana	Tsarist secret police organization
Orgburo	Organizational Bureau, central party organ in charge of personnel and administration, abolished in 1952
partiinost	'party-mindedness'; absolute and unquestioning loyalty to Communist Party policy and ideology
perestroika	'restructuring' – term used to describe Gorbachev's programme of political and economic reform
Politburo	Political Bureau, supreme policy-making body of the Soviet Communist Party
Pravda	literally, 'Truth', the central Bolshevik, later Communist, party newspaper
Proletkult	'Proletarian culture'; campaign in 1920s to promote a specifically industrial working-class culture
rabfak	'workers' faculty'; established in the 1920s to prepare workers and peasants for higher education
Rabkrin	Workers' and Peasants' Inspectorate, organ of state control during 1920s; Stalin was briefly its chairman
Rabochii Put'	'The Workers' Road', Bolshevik party newspaper published during 1917
RSDRP	Russian Social Democratic Workers' Party
soviet	literally, 'council'; since the Revolution, usually referring to central and local government councils
Sovnarkom	Council of People's Commissars – the first Soviet government, set up in October 1917
spetsy	'specialists', especially 'bourgeois specialists', i.e. professionally qualified people employed in various capacities in the 1920s

Yezhovshchina	term applied to Stalin's terror campaign of the 1930s, after Yezhov, head of the NKVD
Zhdanovshchina	term applied to the period of extreme cultural repression in USSR in late 1940s, after senior Politburo member, Andrei Zhdanov

Biographical notes

(names in bold typeface indicate cross-references)

Andropov, Yury Vladimirovich (1914–84). General Secretary of the CPSU (1982–84) and President of the USSR (1983–84). The son of a railway worker, he joined the Communist Party in 1939 and worked his way through the *apparat* holding various posts in the security and diplomatic services. As Soviet Ambassador to Hungary at the time of the Hungarian uprising in 1956, he helped to suppress the insurgency with great ruthlessness. He was head of the KGB from 1967 to 1972, and in 1973 became a full member of **Brezhnev's** Politburo. On Brezhnev's death in 1982, Andropov succeeded him as Party General Secretary. Despite his KGB background and his reputation as something of an intellectual, he made no lasting impression as national leader, and his time as General Secretary simply represents a transition period between Brezhnev's conservative policies and the reforming **Gorbachev**.

Beria, Lavrenty Pavlovich (1899–1953). Georgian Bolshevik with a sinister reputation for ruthless intrigue, duplicity and a voracious sexual appetite. After serving in the Party bureaucracy and security services, he succeeded the disgraced **Yezhov** as head of the NKVD in 1938. During the Second World War he became vice-president of the State Defence Committee, and in 1946 a full member of **Stalin's** Politburo, where he was feared and disliked by his fellow members. Although universally detested, after Stalin's death he briefly became a member of the 'collective leadership' alongside **Malenkov, Khrushchev** and company. Later in 1953 he was arrested in a Kremlin conspiracy, subjected to a brief secret 'trial', and summarily shot.

Brezhnev, Leonid Ilich (1906–82). General Secretary of the CPSU, 1964–82. Born in Ukraine, he joined the Communist Party in 1931 and trained as a metallurgist. In 1938 he became member of the Party *apparat*, and during the Second World War served as a political officer in the Red Army, seeing military action on several fronts (though his wartime exploits were later grossly exaggerated). After the war he served in various senior Party and government posts in Ukraine and Moldavia, and in 1960 was appointed as Chairman of the Praesidium of the Supreme Soviet – that is, titular Head of State. Although a protégé of **Khrushchev**, he was active in the plot to remove the latter from office in 1964, and succeeded him as First (later General) Secretary. Over the next two decades he emerged as the most powerful politician in the Soviet Union, combining his position as General Secretary with that of Head of State in 1977. He took an active role in foreign affairs, maintaining a strong grip on Eastern Europe, but engaging in a policy of détente with the West. His deteriorating health and advancing old age was matched by the declining power of the Soviet Union, increased domestic difficulties and the resultant so-called 'era of stagnation'. On his death in 1982 he was succeeded by the ex-KGB chief, **Andropov**.

Bukharin, Nikolai Ivanovich (1888–1938). Marxist revolutionary theorist and activist in the Bolshevik underground, he took a leading role in the organization of the 1917 October Revolution in Moscow. Described by **Lenin** as 'the darling of the Party', he became a member of the Politburo after the latter's death in 1924. He played a prominent role in the ideological debates of the 1920s and was a strong supporter of what many saw as the pro-peasant New Economic Policy. He was a bitter opponent of **Stalin's** collectivization of agriculture, and in 1937 was arrested during the 'Great Terror'. In 1938 he was placed on public trial, charged with a number of trumped up charges as an 'enemy of the people' and shot. He was formally rehabilitated during **Gorbachev's** *glasnost* campaign, and in 1988 was posthumously readmitted to the Communist Party.

Chernenko, Konstantin Ustinovich (1911–85). A lack-lustre *apparatchik*, Chernenko joined the Communist Party in 1931 and rose through the ranks in various local administrative posts. A close ally of **Brezhnev**, he was elevated to the Politburo in 1978. After failing to secure the succession after the latter's death, he replaced **Andropov** as General Secretary in 1984. His brief tenure of office was unremarkable, and after his death in 1985 he was succeeded by the much younger **Gorbachev**, who embarked on a wide-ranging programme of reform.

Dubček, Alexander (1921–92). Czechoslovak politician and statesman, joined the Communist Party in 1939, rising to the position of First Secretary in 1968. From that position he launched an ambitious programme of internal social, economic and cultural reform – 'the Prague Spring'. The national reform movement was, however, crushed by invading Soviet and other Warsaw Pact forces in August 1968. Dubček was arrested and later expelled from the Communist Party. After a popular uprising and the collapse of the Communist government in 1989, he was elected President of the Czechoslovak parliament. The suppression of the Prague Spring led to the formulation of the neo-Stalinist '**Brezhnev** doctrine', the principle of which was that the Soviet Union had the right to interfere in the internal affairs of other socialist countries when its own interests were believed to be threatened.

Gorbachev, Mikhail Sergeevich (1931–). Soviet politician and statesman, studied at Moscow State University and joined the Communist Party in 1952. He ascended through the ranks of the Party bureaucracy until being appointed to the ailing **Brezhnev's** Politburo in 1980. He finally became General Secretary of the CPSU after the death of **Chernenko** in 1985. He immediately embarked on a radical programme of domestic reform, which included greater freedom of expression and information (*glasnost*) and economic, social and cultural change (*perestroika*). He also called for a thorough revision of the Soviet Union's own history. In foreign affairs his greatest achievements were the ending of Soviet military intervention in Afghanistan, nuclear arms reduction and a policy of non-intervention in the internal affairs of Eastern Europe. Despite his good intentions, the Soviet Union was rapidly moving towards a state of internal disintegration, and in December 1991 he was forced to resign following the suspension of the Communist Party and the collapse of the USSR.

Ivan IV ('the Terrible') (1530–84). Grand Prince of Moscow (1533–84), first Russian ruler to adopt the title 'Tsar' (1547, from Latin 'Caesar'). After defeating the Tatar khanates of Kazan and Astrakhan, he expanded Muscovite power eastwards across Siberia, but was less successful in his wars in the west. Domestically he launched a programme of social reform that was implemented with the ruthless ferocity which earned him his sobriquet, 'the Terrible'. Despite his awesome reputation and his bloodthirsty methods, he later found many admirers, including **Stalin**, who regarded him as a powerful, patriotic and progressive leader.

Kamenev, Lev Borisovich (1883–1936). Leading Bolshevik activist and editor of the Party newspaper *Pravda* in 1917. On the eve of the October Revolution, he and **Zinoviev** argued unsuccessfully on the Central Committee that the uprising should be postponed until elections were held for a Constituent Assembly. During the 1920s he was a member of the Politburo, but was later expelled and finally executed during **Stalin's** purges of the 1930s. He was rehabilitated in 1988.

Kerensky, Alexander Fyodorovich (1881–1970). Lawyer and moderate socialist politician. After the February 1917 Revolution he became a member of both the first Provisional Government (Minister of Justice) and the Executive Committee of the Petrograd Soviet. He eventually became Prime Minister of the third Provisional Government that was overthrown by the Bolsheviks during the October Revolution. He spent the rest of his life in emigration, a bitter opponent of the Soviet regime.

Khrushchev, Nikita Sergeevich (1894–1971). Soviet politician and statesman, born into a peasant family and received little formal education. He joined the Bolshevik (later Communist) Party in 1918 and fought in the Red Army during the Civil War. He supported **Stalin** during the factional struggles of the 1920s, and rose through the Party *apparat* until, having survived the purges, he was appointed member of the Politburo in 1939. Following **Stalin's** death in 1953, he became First Secretary of the Party. He made his mark at the 20th Party Congress in 1956 when he denounced Stalin and the 'cult of personality' in his astounding 'secret speech'. His ambiguous and vacillating policies in office encompassed a limited cultural thaw, economic and sometimes confusing administrative reforms, and a vigorous foreign policy that included the suppression of the Hungarian uprising (1956), the building of the Berlin wall (1961) and the Cuban missile crisis (1962). His shifting policies and his mercurial temperament provoked hostility from other members of the Politburo, and he was ousted from office in a 'Kremlin *coup*' in 1964. He spent the rest of his life in comfortable retirement.

Kirov, Sergei Mironovich (1886–1934). Bolshevik revolutionary and Communist Party politician, played an active role in the October 1917 Revolution and Civil War. A popular figure in the Party, in 1934 he became member of the Politburo and a Secretary of the Central Committee. He was regarded by some as a possible rival to **Stalin**. In December 1934 he was assassinated near his Leningrad headquarters, his death generally being seen as the event that triggered the great purges. Controversy still surrounds the circumstances of his murder, which some commentators believe may have been instigated by Stalin.

Lenin, Vladimir Ilich (1870–1924). Born V. I. Ulyanov, he became a Marxist revolutionary leader. In 1903 he caused a split in the Russian Social Democratic Party between the Bolshevik and Menshevik factions by his insistence on strict discipline, centralization and the role of the Party as 'vanguard of the proletariat'. In April 1917 he returned to Petrograd from exile in Switzerland and immediately called for the overthrow of the 'bourgeois' Provisional Government and the transfer of 'All Power to the Soviets'. Together with **Trotsky** he organized the October Revolution, which overthrew **Kerensky's** Provisional Government and created the first Soviet socialist government, in which **Stalin** became People's Commissar for Nationalities. After the end of the Civil War in 1921 he introduced the New Economic Policy, which some of his comrades regarded as a compromise with capitalism. Shortly before his death, he warned the members of the Party Central Committee of Stalin's growing bureaucratic power, and proposed that he be removed from office as General Secretary. After his death in 1924 his body was embalmed and placed on public display in a mausoleum on Red Square, where it still lies. Stalin quickly orchestrated a 'cult' of Lenin which he manipulated to his own political advantage.

Lysenko, Trofim Denisovich (1898–1976). Russian biologist, creator of a spurious 'scientific' theory that plant-life could be environmentally conditioned, and their acquired characteristics genetically inherited. Although the results of his falsified experiments had no scientific validity, they were politically expedient, and he was supported in his fraudulent views by **Stalin**. As a result, many world-renowned Russian geneticists who criticized him were disgraced or imprisoned, and Soviet genetics, biology and agriculture were set back by a whole generation. His views were not officially repudiated until 1965, when he was finally exposed as a charlatan.

Malenkov, Georgy Maximilianovich (1902–88). Communist Party politician, joined the Party in 1920 and played an active role in implementing the collectivization of the peasants and in the purges of the late 1930s. He became a full member of the Politburo in 1946, and on **Stalin's** death in 1953 succeeded him as First Party Secretary. He was also Prime Minister, but was forced to give up both positions in 1953 and 1955, respectively. However, he remained a member of the post-Stalin collective leadership until forced out of office by **Khrushchev** in 1957 as a member of the so-called 'anti-party group'. Thereafter he was sent to be the manager of a hydroelectric station in Kazakhstan.

Molotov, Vyacheslav Mikhailovich (1890–1986). Born V. M. Skryabin, he was a Party politician and statesman, best known as **Stalin's** People's Commissar for Foreign Affairs at the signing of the Soviet–Nazi Pact of Non-Aggression in 1939 (often known as the Molotov–Ribbentrop Pact). He was also present at the end-of-war conferences of Teheran, Yalta and Potsdam. Despite his wife's imprisonment (she was a Jewess), Molotov managed to survive and serve in some of the highest Party and government posts. He was a prominent member of the post-Stalin collective leadership and an active proponent of an aggressive Soviet foreign policy during the Cold War. He was eventually sacked by **Khrushchev** in 1957 as a member of the 'anti-party group' and dispatched as Soviet Ambassador to Outer Mongolia.

Morozov, Pavel Trofimovich ('Pavlik') (1918–32). Young boy allegedly murdered by his 'kulak' uncle after denouncing his own father to the authorities for illegal activities during the collectivization campaign. Although Pavlik Morozov became something of a cult figure, the full authenticity of the story has been recently questioned.

Nagy, Imre (1895–1958). Hungarian politician, Communist and Prime Minister (1953–56). Active in the Hungarian Soviet Republic of 1919, he fled to Russia in 1929, returning to Hungary with the Red Army in 1944. He became Prime Minister in 1953, and in 1956, following **Khrushchev's** denunciation of **Stalin** at the 20th Congress of the CPSU, lent his support to the Hungarian uprising against Soviet rule. Soviet troops brutally crushed the insurgency, and Nagy was arrested and shot.

Nicholas I (1796–1855). Emperor of Russia (1825–55). His reign was marked by a harsh brand of military-style authoritarianism, strict discipline and intellectual obscurantism that caused his regime to be dubbed 'the apogee of absolutism'. Some have seen his oppressive policies and police methods as a precursor of Stalinist totalitarianism.

Nicholas II (1868–1918). Last Emperor of Russia (1894–1917). Although a staunch upholder of autocratic government, his reign was marked by a series of social, economic and political upheavals that eventually exploded in revolution (1905 and 1917). Against the background of Russia's military failure during the First World War, and faced with mounting popular unrest, he was forced to abdicate in March 1917. Placed under house arrest, he and his family were shot by Bolshevik guards in July 1918. He has since been canonized by the Russian Orthodox Church.

Peter I ('the Great') (1672–1725). Russian Tsar (1682–1721) and first Emperor of Russia (1721–25). One of the most pivotal and controversial figures in Russian history, Peter is best known for his programme of military, administrative, financial, religious and cultural reforms that transformed medieval Muscovy into a major European power. Although many regard his reforms as essential for Russia's survival and modernization, they were enforced with terrifying brutality. Despite being generally feared and detested by his contemporaries, Peter's firmness, vision and energy found him many later admirers, including **Stalin**, with whom he has often been compared.

Putin, Vladimir Vladimirovich (1952–). Ex-KGB officer, politician and current President of the Russian Federation. He was first appointed as acting president by his predecessor, Boris Yeltsin, in 1999 and confirmed in office after presidential elections in 2000. In March 2004 he was re-elected for a second term with such an overwhelming majority as to raise doubts in some quarters over the probity of the electoral procedure. Some have voiced concerns about signs of increasing centralization and presidential control under his regime, which threaten Russia's shaky experiment with democracy after the collapse of the Soviet Union. However, attempts to compare his power with that of **Stalin** are fanciful.

Rykov, Aleksei Ivanovich (1881–1938). Revolutionary Marxist and Soviet politician. In 1924 he succeeded Lenin as Chairman of the Soviet of People's Commissars (i.e. head of government). He sided with **Bukharin** in opposing collectivization and fell foul of Stalin. In 1937 he was arrested during the great purge, tried for treason and sentenced to be shot.

Sakharov, Andrei Dmitrievich (1921–89). Physicist and 'father' of the Soviet hydrogen bomb. During the 1970s he became a leading supporter of nuclear disarmament and an outspoken champion of civil rights in the USSR. In 1975 he was awarded the Nobel Peace Prize, and in 1980 banished by the Soviet authorities to the provincial town of Gorky. In 1986 **Gorbachev** recalled him to Moscow where he was elected a member of the USSR Congress of People's Deputies.

Solzhenitsyn, Alexander Isaevich (1918–). Russian writer and acknowledged leader of the 'dissident movement' during the late 1960s and 1970s. An ex-prison camp inmate and author of such well-known works as *One Day in the Life of Ivan Denisovich, Cancer Ward, The First Circle* and *The Gulag Archipelago*, he was awarded the Nobel Prize for Literature in 1970. He was exiled from the USSR in 1974 and lived for the next twenty years in Vermont, USA. He was allowed to return to Russia in 1994, where he still lives.

Stakhanov, Aleksei Grigorevich (1906–77). Donbas coalminer who in 1934 exceeded his output norm by fourteen times. His achievement was given full publicity treatment, and he became a model for heroic industrial production. The terms 'Stakhanovite' and 'Stakhanovism' have become synonymous with such feats of egregious over-fulfilment. The whole campaign was later exposed as an elaborate hoax based on fraudulent statistics.

Stalin, Joseph Vissarionovich (1878–1953). Born I. V. Djugashvili; Georgian Bolshevik and revolutionary activist; member of the underground party's Central Committee; expert on nationality affairs and close follower of **Lenin**. After the 1917 October Revolution he became People's Commissar for Nationalities, and in 1922 was appointed General Secretary of the Communist Party. Further details of his career as virtual dictator of the Soviet Union are contained throughout this book.

Tito, Josip Broz (1892–1980). Yugoslav Communist, wartime partisan and politician. After the end of the Second World War Tito (then Marshal Tito) became Yugoslavia's first communist Prime Minister, consolidating his authority with the presidency in 1953. His position at home was powerful enough for him to break with **Stalin** in 1948 and pursue an independent Yugoslav style of communism with an emphasis on workers' control. In foreign affairs Yugoslavia played a leading role in the association of non-aligned countries. Tito was made president for life in 1974.

Trotsky, Lev Davidovich (1879–1940). Born L. D. Bronstein; Marxist revolutionary polemicist and activist, developed his 'theory of permanent revolution' (which in the 1920s conflicted with Stalin's theory of 'Socialism in One Country'). He joined the Bolshevik Party in July 1917, and became leader of the Military Revolutionary Committee of the Petrograd Soviet, playing a major role in the planning and organization of the October revolution. He was Commissar for War and organizer of the Red Army during the Civil War. His political rivalry with **Stalin** after the death of **Lenin** led to his expulsion from the Soviet Union (1929), and his later assassination in Mexico by one of Stalin's agents.

Vyshinsky, Andrei Yanuarevich (1883–1954). Russian jurist and politician, born in Odessa. A former Menshevik, he joined the Communist Party in 1920 and became professor of criminal law and Attorney General. He was the chief prosecutor in the notorious show trials (1936–38) that eliminated most of Stalin's rivals. In court he displayed a hectoring, sneering and abusive manner that aimed to humiliate the accused whom he constantly vilified in the most sickening terms. He almost invariably demanded the death penalty. He later went on to a diplomatic career, including a brief spell as Foreign Minister (1949–53).

Yagoda, Genrikh Grigorevich (1891–1938). Born Heinrich Yehuda, joined the Bolshevik Party in 1907. In 1920 he became a member of the Cheka (see Glossary), rising to be head of the NKVD in 1934. In that position he organized the early stages of **Stalin's** purges, including the public show trial of **Zinoviev**, **Kamenev** and others. He was himself later arrested and replaced by **Yezhov**. In 1938 he appeared alongside **Bukharin** in the last of the show trials and was sentenced to be shot.

Yezhov, Nikolai Ivanovich (1895–1939). Took over from **Yagoda** as head of the NKVD in 1936; known as 'the poison dwarf', he lent his name to the most bloody period of **Stalin's** purges, the *Yezhovshchina*. After the last of the show trials in 1938, he was demoted to the position of People's Commissar for Water Transport, and replaced at the NKVD by **Beria**. He was later arrested and disappeared, presumably shot.

Zhdanov, Andrei Alexandrovich (1896–1948). Communist Party politician, joined the Bolshevik Party in 1915. After a career in the Party central and local bureaucracy, he succeeded the murdered **Kirov** as chief of the Leningrad Party organization (1934) and was elected to the Politburo in 1939. Between 1946 and 1948 he became **Stalin's** chief 'hatchet man' in the philistine campaign for strict cultural, artistic and literary conformity, tinged with overt anti-Semitism, which was to bear his name – the *Zhdanovschina*. His death in 1948 allowed his rivals to launch a minor purge of Zhdanov's protégés, usually known as the 'Leningrad affair'.

Zhukov, Georgy Konstantinovich (1896–1974). Brilliant military commander and veteran of many decisive battles during the Great Patriotic War (e.g. Moscow, Stalingrad, Kursk, Warsaw, Berlin). Four times Hero of the Soviet Union he was promoted Marshal in 1943 and accepted the German surrender at Karlshorst on 9 May 1945. Despite Zhukov's popularity and his military successes, **Stalin** was always suspicious of him and sought to distance him from too much political influence. After Stalin's death he returned to Moscow as Deputy Minister of Defence, and then as Minister of Defence (1955). **Khrushchev** dismissed him from the latter post in 1957, suspecting him of 'Bonapartism'. A large equestrian statue of Zhukov now stands near the northern entrance to Red Square in Moscow.

Zinoviev, Grigory Evseevich (1883–1936). Marxist revolutionary and close associate of **Lenin**, with whom, however, he disagreed over the staging of the Bolshevik-led workers' armed uprising in October 1917. They settled their differences after the Revolution, and **Zinoviev** became President of the Communist International. After Lenin's death in 1924 he initially sided with **Stalin** in opposing **Trotsky's** possible succession to the leadership. During the purges of the 1930s he was arrested and accused of counter-revolutionary activities, convicted in a public show trial and executed in 1936. He was formally rehabilitated under **Gorbachev.**

Index